"I'm Not Good Enough"

Sharon Jaynes

HARVEST HOUSE PUBLISHERS
EUGENE, OREGON

Cover by Garborg Design Works, Savage, Minnesota

"I'M NOT GOOD ENOUGH"...AND OTHER LIES WOMEN TELL THEMSELVES
Copyright © 2009 by Sharon Jaynes
Published by Harvest House Publishers
Eugene, Oregon 97402
www.harvesthousepublishers.com

Library of Congress Cataloging-in-Publication Data
   Jaynes, Sharon.
   "I'm not good enough"-- and other lies women tell themselves / Sharon Jaynes.
      p. cm.
   Includes bibliographical references.
   ISBN 978-0-7369-1870-1 (pbk.)
   ISBN 978-0-7369-3378-0 (eBook)
   1. Women—Religious aspects—Christianity. 2. Self-perception—Religious aspects—Chris-
tianity. 3. Self-esteem—Religious aspects—Christianity. 4. Christian women—Religious life. I.
Title.
   BT704.J35 2009
   248.8'43—dc22

                                                                        2008028528

Printed in the United States of America

13 14 15 16 / VP-SK / 14 13 12 11 10 9

To two of my favorite people in the world,
Mary Southerland and Gwen Smith.
Serving in ministry with you has
been one of my greatest joys.

Acknowledgments

There are so many amazing people who have worked together to make this project possible. A special thanks to the Harvest House family: Bob Hawkins Jr., who continues his father's dream of reaching the world for Christ with the printed word; LaRae Weikert, who has the uncanny ability to make everyone feel like they are her best friend; Terry Glaspey, who is an amazing listener, encourager, and friend; Barb Sherrill, Katie Lane, Rob Teigen, John Constance, Christianne Debysingh, Jeana Newman, Dave Bartlett, and Dave Sheets, who creatively get the message of hope and healing to a hurting world; and Shane White, who makes the Energizer Bunny look as if he's moving in slow motion. I am also grateful for my editor, Rod Morris, for his attention to detail and theological expertise.

＊ ＊ ＊ ＊ ＊

I am especially thankful for two friends who encouraged me on when I felt that I wasn't good enough, my Girlfriends in God: Gwen Smith and Mary Southerland. I'm also forever thankful for my prayer team—Van Walton, Christie Legg, Barbara Givens, Kathy Mendietta, Gayle Montgomery, Linda Butler, Bonnie Schulte, Cynthia Price, Naomi Gingerich, and Linda Eppley—and for the many friends who shared their stories in order to expose the lies we believe and the truth that sets us free.

＊ ＊ ＊ ＊ ＊

This book would not be a reality without my "in-house editor," my precious husband, Steve. Thank you for believing in me and giving me the love and encouragement I needed to press on.

＊ ＊ ＊ ＊ ＊

Most of all, I am thankful for my Heavenly Father who loves me, the Holy Spirit who empowers me, and my Savior, Jesus Christ, who set me free.

Contents

House of Mirrors

*I have no greater joy than to hear that my
children are walking in the truth.*

3 JOHN 4

Carrie stood before the bathroom mirror putting the finishing touches on her makeup before rushing off to the county fair with her girlfriends. Just a bit of lip gloss and one more swipe of the hairbrush and she was ready to go.

Carrie heard the horn blow as the girls pulled in the driveway, and she grabbed her sweater and yelled to her mom still in the kitchen.

"Bye mom, I'll be home by eleven."

"Be careful," her mom called out.

Carrie, Katie, Clair, and Meghan scurried from booth to booth as the carnival barkers drew them in. They watched boys humiliate themselves with attempts to fire rifles at metal foxes running across a black backdrop, shoot basketballs into hoops that seemed strangely small, and bang a giant hammer to prove who was the strongest among the bunch. The girls tried their hands at throwing darts to pop balloons, casting rings over old milk jugs, and tossing balls in slanted straw baskets. After eating a pink sticky cloud of cotton candy, the girls wandered over to various side shows.

"Come one, come all," the barker called. "Step right up and see yourself as you've never been seen before. The House of Mirrors, sure to entertain and amuse. Step right up."

"Come on in, little lady," the dark man with greasy black hair and toothy grin motioned to Carrie. She shivered and wanted to turn and run away.

"Let's go in here," Katie said. "This'll be fun."

Carrie was whisked away with the crowd and lured into the first mirrored room. Elongated reflections stared back, and the girls giggled at the taller, thinner versions of themselves. In the next room, they doubled over in laughter at their stubby arms and legs, expanded torsos, and chubby cheeks. They struck various poses and got a taste of what midget versions of themselves might look like.

The girls then ran to a third room, but Carrie stayed behind. She was silent as she stood mesmerized at what she saw staring back at her. Words began to appear across her chest, fading in and out in various scripted forms. *Worthless. Unloved. Ugly. Stupid. Unacceptable. Unforgivable. Dirty. Unhappy. Failure. Not good enough.*

Was this a trick? Did the others see what she saw? How did they know? Tears began trickling down her cheeks as hidden memories flashed before her.

"Carrie, come on!" Meghan called from down the hall. "Let's go to the bumper cars."

Carrie took a deep breath, put on her perma-smile, and wiped her eyes. No one noticed the mascara trail down her cheeks or the puffy swollen eyes. Like always…no one knew.

House of Mirrors

I was in the sixth grade when I first ventured into the House of Mirrors at my hometown county fair. Like Carrie, my group of giggling friends ran from booth to booth suckered into paying good money to play rigged games. For hours we gave our money to shady carnival characters in hopes of winning a stuffed purple polka-dot snake, oversized tie-dyed teddy bear, or a pair of fuzzy dice to hang from a car's rearview mirror. Personally, I stuck with pickup ducks. A sure win.

We soared into the air on the Ferris wheel to get a good look at the small-town lights, rode through the darkened House of Horrors with a favorite beau, and plunged down the mountainous rickety roller coaster with arms in the air. But of all the side shows at the carnival, it was the house of mirrors that captured my attention.

Like Carrie and her friends, we walked through maze-like halls giggling at the distorted images of ourselves. I looked at the various versions of me and tried to decide which one I liked best. But deep inside, in a place I didn't even know existed, part of me was *truly* in search of another version of me. I did not like the one I knew best.

Because I had no idea who I really was.

Now I have come to realize that many women grow up with a distorted image of who they really are. They look into the mirror of performance and see the words *not good enough.* They stare into the mirror of value and see *worthless.* They peer into the looking glass of success and see *failure.* They gaze into the mirror of competence and see *inferior, insecure,* and *inadequate.*

They live in a house of mirrors believing distorted interpretations of who they are…and it's all a lie.

Broken Mirrors

How did this happen? Where do the lies come from? Why is it so easy to believe the lies about who we are rather than the truth? What *is* the truth? We will look at all these questions and many more throughout our time together. But I will tell you this—it all began in the Garden.

After the sixth day of creation, when God looked at all He made, He said, "It is good." But something went terribly wrong. The enemy crept into God's perfect world and deceived His image bearers with lies. And while God's redemptive plan has restored what the serpent destroyed, the enemy continues to tell us lies even today. He tells us that we are worthless, powerless failures who are not good enough, smart enough, or competent enough to succeed.

And it is not the truth.

When God created the world and stocked the seas with marine life and the skies with winged creatures—when He ignited the stars in the night sky and placed the sun to light the day and the moon to illumine the darkness—He did so with words. *"And God said…"* and it came to be (Genesis 1:3-26). God spoke and what was not became what is.

> By the word of the LORD were the heavens made,
>> their starry host by the breath of his mouth (Psalm 33:6).

Amazingly, when God created man in His own image, He gave us the power of language. He didn't entrust monkeys, zebras, or elephants with words. He gave words to man. Our words also have creative potential. The Bible tells us that "death and life are in the power of the tongue" (Proverbs 18:21 NASB). Our words become the mirror in which others see themselves. Our words affect children, husbands, friends, and the world. But some of the most powerful words we speak are the ones that no one hears…the words we speak to ourselves.

We can speak life to ourselves and we can speak death to ourselves. Our minds think about 130 words per minute and our mouths (women) speak about 25,000 words in a day. That's a lot of words. A considerable amount of those words are spoken or thought to ourselves. Most of this self-talk is harmless, such as *What will I fix for dinner?* or *Where did I put my hairbrush?* But some are very destructive.

Saying, *I'm so stupid, I'm such an idiot,* or *I'm never going to be good enough,* can create habitual destructive thought patterns that can paralyze a person into inactivity. Negative self-perceptions repeated over time will brand themselves into our minds and eventually become our reality. If you repeat a misbelief or lie enough times, you begin to believe it. *Nobody loves me, I don't have any friends,* or *I'm so ugly* becomes your reality…even though it's a false reality. You can become stuck in the house of mirrors looking at a distorted reflection of who you really are.

The negative destructive lies of the enemy are like fly paper. The more you handle it or toy with it, the more you get stuck to it. Each time we speak a lie about ourselves, the more we become bound to it. "For as he thinks within himself, so he is" (Proverbs 23:7 NASB).

God's Mirror

When we look into God's mirror, His incredible love letter to us we call the Bible, we discover the truth. God does love you (Colossians 3:12). You have an entire cloud of witnesses cheering for you (Hebrews 12:1). You are God's masterpiece...a work of beautiful art (Ephesians 2:10). You are good enough because Christ lives in you (John 14:20). You are a chosen, holy, dearly loved child of God. That's the truth. Let's get out of the house of mirrors and start seeing ourselves as God sees us.

In one of John's letters, he wrote, "I have no greater joy than to hear that my children are walking in the truth" (3 John 4). I believe that God has no greater joy than to know that *His* children are walking in the truth. When we are walking in the truth, the lies are exposed. We can recognize the lie, reject the lie, and replace the lie with truth. Then, and only then, can we be all that God has created us to be and do all that God has created us to do. We can experience the abundant life He planned all along.

I believe that God has great plans for all of us—His Word promises that He does.

> "No eye has seen,
>   no ear has heard,
>   no mind has conceived
>   what God has prepared for those who love him"
>   (1 Corinthians 2:9).

But many of us are not experiencing the abundant life because we don't know who we are. We have believed the lies that we are unloved, unworthy, and unforgivable. We have been looking in distorted mirrors far too long. God wants us to look into the only true mirror that will tell us exactly who we are, what we have, and where we are as a child of God—His Word.

It is time to start believing the truth. It is time to hear God say, "You are My daughter, whom I love; with you I am well pleased."

Are you ready to walk out of the house of mirrors once and for all? Are you ready to begin seeing yourself as God sees you? Are you ready to begin living the abundant life that God planned all along?

Let's grab hands and begin the journey of walking in the truth together.

Part 1

The Battle for the Mind

Realize the Enemy's True Identity

*"The thief comes only to steal and kill and destroy; I have
come that they may have life, and have it to the full."*

JOHN 10:10

Mary Beth stood before the bathroom mirror, brushing her
shoulder length hair and staring at the reflection before her. It
seemed like only yesterday she was a carefree little girl swinging from
the monkey bars on the schoolhouse playground. Oh, how she longed
for the days when her greatest concern was which hair bow to wear
in her neatly tied ponytail.

"Mommy, watch this," echoed as the distant memories passed
before her.

Birthday parties with increasing candles, dance recitals with
flashing cameras, prom dresses with handsome escorts, cheerleading
routines with admiring fans, church youth group with open Bibles,
and teary-eyed parents driving away from her college dorm. Then
there was Bob.

"Bob," she whispered as tears pooled in her eyes.

Bob and Mary Beth met at a campus ministry gathering her junior
year. He was everything she had hoped for in a husband: handsome,
ambitious, spiritual, and most of all, attentive. Both sets of parents
beamed as they watched the couple walk down the red-carpeted aisle
of their church after pledging their life-long love.

Fifteen years later, Mary Beth and Bob had a mortgage, three kids,
a dog, busy schedules, and a loveless marriage. They were so busy
taking care of life that they forgot to take care of love.

That's when Jim appeared. She recalled the day she ran into the grocery store to pick up a loaf of bread.

"Mary Beth, is that you?"

"Jim! It's so good to see you," she said as they met halfway down the aisle in a friendly hug. "Where have you been? When did you get back in town?"

"I've been working in Europe for the past ten years," Jim said, "but now I'm back for a while. Man, you look great. Didn't anyone tell you that you're supposed to *look* older as you *get* older? I'd love to catch up. Do you have a minute to step over to Starbucks and grab a cup of coffee?"

Mary Beth's heart quickened. How long had it been since anyone had told her she looked great? She couldn't even remember. "No, I'd better not. I need to get back home."

"Well, maybe next time," Jim said. "I just can't get over how good you look."

"Oh hush," Mary Beth said. "You always were a flatterer. I'll see you around."

Over the next several months, Mary Beth and Jim bumped into each other several times. She even found herself applying lipstick and making sure her hair looked nice before leaving the house just in case she saw him. Her mind began to daydream about what it would be like to share a candlelight dinner with Jim. She imagined him reaching for her hand or brushing a stray strand of hair from her face.

Mary Beth knew in her heart that the imaginings were not healthy. This had to stop. So she planned a special surprise for Bob, hoping a romantic evening would suppress or replace the longings she felt for Jim.

She recalled the evening. The kids were at a neighbor's house for the evening, the dinner was cooked to perfection, and the candlelit room wafted with lavender fragrance. All day long Mary Beth had prepared. The clingy low-cut dress was intentional, not to mention what was underneath. Her hair was just like he liked it, and her body was scented, softened, and waiting to be touched.

"Hello," Mary Beth answered when the phone rang.

"Hi, honey. Listen, I'm not going to be able to make it home on time tonight. I might not even make it home at all. I've got an emergency meeting with the board, and it looks like we're going to be on a conference call until morning. Seems like our China export deal is in jeopardy. We didn't have anything planned tonight, did we?"

"No," was all she said.

"OK, see you later." Click.

I can't believe he just did that. All he cares about is work. I can't live like this any longer. This isn't a marriage, it's job share. I tried. It didn't work. I can't believe God wants me to live like this. I know He wants more for me.

Mary Beth walked over to her pocketbook and searched for the business card with a number scribbled on the back.

"Hello," Jim answered.

"Hi, Jim. This is Mary Beth. Are you still up for that cup of coffee?"

There were many cups of coffee and planned meetings after that evening. Three months later, Mary Beth and Jim consummated their affair.

Temptation had turned into condemnation. The forbidden fruit had rotted in her soul, and she wanted to die.

Looking down at the bottle of sleeping pills the doctor had prescribed, she thought just how easy it would be to end it all…right now…today.

The Enemy's Plot

I wish I could tell you that this is a script from *Desperate Housewives*, but it's not. It's a common tale that I hear time and time again. The names change, but the story line remains the same. And it makes me mad. I'm not angry at the women who pour their hearts out to me, but I am mad at the enemy who lies to them. The enemy who whispers that God is holding out on them—that they could be happy if only…

And it's nothing new. This is the same old story that began in the Garden of Eden with the same antagonist deceiving the leading lady into his dungeon of doom. But I'm getting ahead of myself. Let's start at the very beginning.

Five days after time began, the Creator of the universe gazed at all He had made and was not completely satisfied. Yes, as the sun set on each of the first five days on God's kingdom calendar, He said, "It is good." But there was something missing. Something more. Someone more.

The stage was set for Act 6. The curtain rose. Everything had to be perfect for God's grand finale. The angels gathered round as God announced the final scene on the grand drama of "In the Beginning."

God began with an announcement: "Let us make man in our image." This being will be different from all the rest. With body, soul, and spirit, man will enter into a relationship with the Creator on a personal and intimate level. He will be just a little lower than the angels and rule over the animals, birds, and fish. Man will be God's friend.

So God knelt on the ground and gathered a handful of dirt. He spat on the dust and began forming the most magnificent creation to date. With His very fingertips, God fashioned man's inward parts: capillaries, nerve endings, brain cells, hair follicles, eyelashes, taste buds. Meticulously and deliberately, the Artist created a masterpiece of divine design.

And as the lifeless form lay before the celestial audience, God placed His mouth upon the nostrils of man and breathed life into his waiting lungs. Man's heart began to beat, the lungs began to expand, and the eyes began to flutter open. And the curtain began to fall on this, the sixth day of creation.

"Wait!" the Creator said. "My work is not done. It is not good for man to be alone. I will create a helper suitable for him. A companion like him, but yet, oh so different."

So God—the Us, the three-in-one—began to fashion the grand finale...woman.

Can't you just see it now? Can't you sense the excitement of the angels as they hovered low? From the very beginning of time, mankind was set apart. Man and woman were uniquely designed for a specific purpose as God's image bearers to rule the earth.

But there was one among the onlookers that day who watched with evil intent. Yes, he was among the created angelic beings, one of the most beautiful, in fact. But he wasn't happy with God's creation. Earlier, this angelic being decided he didn't like his position in the heavenly order. He wanted to elevate himself above God. And while he had been created to be a light-bearer, his rebellion caused him to be thrown to the earth to become known as the Prince of Darkness.

And now there were these...*humans*...created in God's image. The enemy was not pleased. As soon as Adam and Eve stood on the stage, the Prince of Darkness began to devise their demise. If he was going down, he was going to take as many of these image bearers with him as possible.

Adam and Eve lived in a perfect world. All their needs were cared for. They had perfect communion with God and with each other. They were "naked and felt no shame." The only restriction placed on them was that they were not to eat from the tree of the knowledge of good and evil located in the middle of the Garden. God warned Adam, "When you eat of it you will surely die."

As they basked in the light of God's love, darkness slithered into the Garden with his plan to steal, kill, and destroy the image bearers. And how did he do it? He did it with the most powerful weapon of all...lies.

The Enemy's Lies

"Now the serpent..." The great deceiver clothed himself as a serpent and slithered up to Eve with a game plan to destroy God's prized possession. He didn't come with a sword or a gun or even a knife for his attack. He simply wielded lies.

The serpent knew Adam and Eve would not buy into a barefaced denial of God, so he slithered into the garden with a twist and a turn of the truth. He began by causing Eve to doubt. "Did God really say, 'You must not eat from any tree in the garden'?" (Genesis 3:1).

Satan knew *exactly* what God had said. He was simply trying to confuse Eve. Perhaps he was evaluating just how well she knew the truth. He found out.

"We may eat fruit from the trees in the garden," Eve replied, "but God did say, 'You must not eat fruit from the tree that is in the middle of the garden, and you must not touch it, or you will die'" (v. 3).

Bingo. She didn't know the truth that well after all. God never mentioned not touching the fruit. That seems like a pretty good idea, but it was not what God said.

Now Satan didn't even try to disguise the deception. He told a flat-out lie. "You will *not* surely die." (v. 4).

And finally, he told her she could be like God. "For God knows that when you eat of it your eyes will be opened, and you will be like God, knowing good and evil" (v. 5). In other words, "God doesn't know what He's talking about. He's holding out on you. You don't need Him. You can be your own god."

Eve rejected the truth and believed the lie. She believed that she could be like God, in control of her own life. "When the woman saw that the fruit of the tree was good for food and pleasing to the eye, and also desirable for gaining wisdom, she took some and ate it. She also gave some to her husband, who was with her, and he ate it" (v. 6).

And as she sank her teeth into the forbidden fruit of deception, it settled in her soul and fermented into shame and condemnation. Her husband also felt the sickening rot of sin settle in his soul. Suddenly shame and fear entered the world, and Adam and Eve hid from God like wayward children.

All temptation is an attempt to get us to live our lives independent of God. Satan is not very creative, but he is very effective. And he has been lying to us ever since. Why? Because it works.

Every one of his lies springs from the idea that happiness is just a decision away. Satan wants you to believe God is holding out on you. You can be like God. You can be your own god. Rather than being thankful for what we do have, he points out what we don't have. Think about it. Eve had at her disposal every tree in the garden except one. Every tree. That is a smorgasbord of goodness. But rather than being thankful, she bought the lie that the one thing she couldn't have was the one thing that would make her happy. *I would be happy if...* Is any of this sounding familiar to you? It should. Satan uses the same tactics with us that he used with Eve.

Eve believed the enemy's lie over God's truth. His plan worked. But what the serpent did not know was that God's amazing plan of forgiveness and grace was about to unfold. Satan did not win the battle for man's soul in the garden. Jesus Christ won the war on Calvary's Cross. When Jesus said, "It is finished," and breathed His last, He made a way for all mankind to regain all that Adam and Eve had lost.

The Consequence of Sin

After Adam and Eve ate from the tree of the knowledge of good and evil, they realized they were naked and were ashamed. So they hid.

In the cool of the day, when God came to stroll with His friends, they were nowhere to be seen. Of course He knew where they were. He always does. But He called out anyway, "Where are you?"

Adam and Eve appeared from behind the bushes clothed in fig leaves and a downcast countenance. They admitted what they had done...sort of. Adam blamed the disobedience on Eve, Eve blamed her actions on Satan, and Satan...well, I imagine he just grinned from pointy ear to pointy ear.

God cursed the serpent and predicted that One would come to crush his head. The consequences of Adam's sin were increased toil in working the ground, but with little result. The consequences of Eve's sin were increased pain in childbirth and her husband would now rule over her. But the most painful punishment of all was separation from God and spiritual death.

Adam and Eve were cast out of the Garden of Eden. Cherubim with flaming swords were placed at the entrance to keep them out. I can almost hear Eve as she walked out of the garden down the path of failure and defeat. *How did this happen? What have I done? How could I have been so foolish?* Tell me, haven't you wondered the same after you've bought the enemy's lies and succumbed to his suggestions?

Just yesterday she had it all. It was a time of firsts. "In the beginning" quickly shone the spotlight on Eve: the first woman, the first wife, the first to believe the enemy's lies. Oh yes, she was a woman of many firsts, but she would not be the last.

The Savior's Plan

Thankfully, God made sure that *how it happened* was recorded in great detail so that we can learn from Eve's mistakes and be prepared when the enemy attacks us as well. Satan still peddles the forbidden fruit, and his goal is the same as it was in the beginning of time—steal, kill, and destroy (John 10:10). Just as army commanders study an enemy's tactics, God has given us the enemy's battle plan for close examination. From Genesis to Revelation we can examine what he does and how he does it so that we will not be "unaware of his schemes" (2 Corinthians 2:11).

And here's the good news. The battle has already been won. Jesus came to destroy the devil's work (1 John 3:8) and destroy it He did. We simply need to know the truth, believe the truth, and walk in the truth of what Jesus has already accomplished for us on the cross.

A man in the Arizona desert came upon a diamondback rattlesnake. With a hoe in the back of his trunk, he killed the rattler and cut off his head. Amazingly, the headless snake continued to shake his rattle and lunge at him. "What's worse," the man said, "even though I knew its head was cut off, that he was dead, I still flinched."[1]

Satan's head has been cut off. He has already lost the battle but continues to shake his rattle to draw our attention away from the truth of his defeat. And while he has been defeated, he wants us to think he is still in control.

In a nutshell, here's the truth we need to latch on to: God created man in His image. Satan deceived man with a lie that he could be like God. Man traded the truth for the lie and while his body lived for a time, and his soul lived for eternity, his spirit died totally and completely at the very moment of disobedience. Every person born since that time has been born with a live body and soul but a dead spirit (Romans 5:12; see also Ephesians 2:1; 1 Corinthians 15:21-22). But just as soon as Eve's teeth sank into the forbidden fruit, the shadow of the cross appeared on the horizon. All of the Old Testament points to that defining moment on the hill of Calvary when Jesus broke the chains of hell that had us bound and set us free from the penalty of sin.

When we accept Jesus Christ as our Savior and make Him Lord of our lives, we experience new birth—we become a new creation (2 Corinthians 5:17). Not only do we receive the promise of heaven for all eternity, we receive a new identity that day.

When we understand who we are in Christ, where we are in Christ, and what we have in Christ, we walk in victory through the storms of life, in abundance through the desert days, and in freedom in the confines of earth.[2]

But friend, Satan does not give up on you when you become a Christian. He knows who you are, what you have, and where you are as a child of God. He knows that you are chosen, accepted, adopted, appointed, valuable, justified, reconciled, redeemed, righteous, free from condemnation, holy, sealed, complete, and completely forgiven. His mission is to keep you from walking in the truth of who you are, and he uses the same tactics today that he used with Eve. That's why it's so important to understand what happened in the Garden. We must recognize Satan's tactics in order to fight the battle for our minds.

Paul exhorts us to "put on the full armor of God so that [we] can take [our] stand against the devil's schemes" (Ephesians 6:11), but Christians often operate like "blindfolded warriors. Not knowing who our enemy is, we strike out at each other."[3] Let's take a look at who this enemy really is.

The Enemy Revealed

Who exactly is Satan? His name means "adversary, one who resists."

He is a created being. Just as God created man, He also created Satan. Oh, He didn't create the evil one as we know him today. He created an angel named Lucifer, which means "morning star." However, Lucifer, like man, also had a free will. At some point he chose to rebel against God and was thrown from heaven with one-third of the angels. We aren't told the exact details of Lucifer's fall from heaven, but two prophets, Ezekiel and Isaiah, have alluded to it (Ezekiel 28:12-17; Isaiah 14:12-15).

One thing we do know for sure, Jesus said, "I saw Satan fall like lightning from heaven" (Luke 10:18). Jesus was there. We must always remember that while Jesus came to earth in bodily form at a certain point in history, He *was* before history began. "In the beginning was the Word, and the Word was with God, and the Word was God. He was with God in the beginning" (John 1:1). Jesus was. Jesus is. Jesus always will be.

When Satan was thrown from heaven he wanted to take more than one-third of the angels with him into the final condemnation that is coming in the last days. And he wanted to take along as many human souls as possible.

The enemy has many aliases: the ruler of demons (Luke 11:12), the god of this world (2 Corinthians 4:4), the prince of the power of the air (2 Corinthians 2:2), the accuser (Revelation 12:10), the father of lies (John 8:44), the deceiver (Genesis 3:13), the great dragon (Revelation 12:9), the ancient serpent (Revelation 12:9), the devil (Revelation 12:9), and Satan, who leads the whole world astray (Revelation 12:9). Each one of these names reveals something about his nature and tactics.

"Scripture depicts him opposing God's work (Zechariah 3:1), perverting God's Word (Matthew 4:6), hindering God's servant (1 Thessalonians 2:18), obscuring the gospel (2 Corinthians 4:4), snaring the righteous (1 Timothy 3:7), and holding the world in his power (1 John 5:19)."[4] Satan cannot dwell in a true believer because a true believer is sealed by and inhabited by the Holy Spirit. However, he can taunt, tempt, and trouble a believer by putting ideas and thoughts into the mind. He masks his thoughts as our own thoughts in order to get us to act in disobedience to God's will. However, he cannot *make* us do anything. It is always our choice. He simply makes the suggestion.

The World

My brother was about four years old when he decided to grab a box of matches and a handful of sparklers to see how they worked. He had heard that sparklers worked best in the dark, so he went into the darkest place he could find at Grandma's house...her wardrobe closet.

My brother snuck into the darkness, crouched amongst the dresses and coats, and lit the first match. The sparklers immediately began shooting fiery sparks in all directions. Within moments, Stewart noticed more than sparklers on fire. Grandma's clothes were up in flames. (I'm happy to say that Stewart wasn't harmed, unless you count the spanking he got from Grandma.)

Friends, we don't have to go into a closet to find the darkness. It's waiting for us the moment we step out the front door, turn on the television, or listen to the six o'clock news. The world is full of darkness at every turn. Satan is not our only enemy. The Bible tells us that our struggle is against the world, the flesh, and the devil.

What exactly is *the world?* In the Bible there are several definitions. Sometimes *world* refers to all the people on the earth: "For God so loved the *world* that he gave his one and only Son" (John 3:16). In some instances *world* refers to planet earth itself. At other times *world* refers to the world's values and mores. It is this worldliness that Paul refers to when he says, "Do not conform any longer to the pattern of this *world*" (Romans 12:2). Jesus said that the world hated Him and we shouldn't be surprised if it hates us as well (John 15:18-19). Both refer to the world's values or ways of thinking.

The Bible also tells us that "the whole world is under the control of the evil one" (1 John 5:19). It seems as though we are splitting hairs here. But when we consider the power of the enemy and the pull of the world systems, they are almost one and the same. Right now, the world systems are being heavily influenced by the evil one.

But here's the hope. Jesus said, "But take heart! I have overcome the world" (John 16:33). As long as we live in the world, we will feel its pull. But God assures us that we have what it takes to "overcome the world" (1 John 5:4-5). We have the power of the Holy Spirit living in us and faith in the Victor who works through us.

The Flesh

One more enemy in this battle for our minds is the flesh. From the time we are born, we receive messages about ourselves—some true, some false. We go through our lives doing whatever we think necessary to feel safe, secure, and significant. Between the time we are born physically and the time we are born spiritually (born again), we form certain habit patterns and thought patterns. Our unique way of getting our God-given needs met on our own strength and by our own means is our unique version of the flesh.

As with the word *world*, *flesh* has several meanings in the Bible. One meaning is simply our bodies—our literal flesh and bones. The Bible says "The Word became flesh and made his dwelling among us" (John 1:14). Jesus came in bodily form—flesh and blood.

But there is another use of *flesh* that refers to our sinful thought patterns and actions that develop over time. It is our mechanism for getting our needs met apart from God. Once we become a Christian, the desire to do things our way and in our strength apart from God does not instantly go away. No one pushes the delete button on our old programming. Now there is a struggle between the flesh, with its default button of selfish thought patterns and actions, and the spirit with its desire to please God.

When we come to Jesus Christ, we are born again and have a new spirit within us. We are saved from the penalty of sin. However, as long as we live in an earthly body, we will battle with the power of sin. Our old fleshly desires war against our new spiritual desires. While we fight battles with the world on the outside, we also fight battles with the flesh on the inside—our mind, will, and emotions.

I live on a lake, and we are blessed and plagued with various winged fowl. Occasionally, we are invaded by Canadian geese. Strangely, some of the confused travelers have stopped mid-flight and decided that shopping center parking lots are fabulous places to start a family. So Momma and Papa Goose scoop out a nest under a tree and proceed to lay eggs. Momma does her job of sitting on the eggs, and Papa does his job of protecting his family. He squawks and spits at shoppers simply minding their business, charges curious kids, and struts around as if he owns the place.

One day I watched as a gander waddled over to a minivan and began furiously attacking a hubcap. The confused fowl saw his reflection and had no idea he was fighting himself and just about broke his beak.

Now, friend, we need to learn how to replace the lies with the truth and "out truth" the enemy, but sometimes we need to realize that we are fighting against our own poor choices and weaknesses. Sure Satan notices and takes advantages of those weaknesses. That's how any opponent makes his conquest. But we have to take responsibility for our fleshly choices and admit our sins, confess our mistakes, and repent—turn and go in the opposite direction.

The world, the flesh, and the devil are so intertwined that they can hardly be separated. Ultimately, Satan is the chief conductor driving the train of lies, and he's driving it right off a cliff. But remember, he can never *make* you do anything. We always have a choice. God always provides a way of escape (1 Corinthians 10:13).

The Victory

We never have to go looking for trouble. We don't need to pick a fight with the enemy. Jesus defeated Satan on the cross of Calvary, not by confronting him openly, but by fulfilling the destiny He had been called to. Likewise, we defeat the enemy every time we choose God's truth over a lie, obey God's commands over our desires, and walk in faith rather than run in fear.

"The greatest battle that was ever won was accomplished by the apparent death of the victor, without even a word of rebuke to His adversary! The prince of this world was judged and principalities and powers were disarmed not by confrontational warfare, but by the surrender of Jesus on the cross."[5]

The Bible describes Satan as a roaring lion seeking someone to devour. A lion roars in order to frighten his prey. But we don't need to be afraid. This lion, even though he may roar, has no teeth, and I've never heard of an animal that can gum his prey to death.

The purpose of this chapter is to expose the enemy's true identity. However, the enemy is never to be our focus. Our focus is on the Victorious Savior, God's only Son, who defeated the enemy on the cross. Jesus Christ reigns supreme, and ministering angels surround us on every side (Hebrews 1:14). Greater is He that is in you than he that is in the world (1 John 4:4).

> Turn your eyes upon Jesus,
> Look full in His wonderful face,
> And the things of earth will grow strangely dim,
> In the light of His glory and grace.
>   (Helen H. Lemmel)

Now we know the enemy's true identity. But more importantly, we know the Savior who has defeated him.

3

Recognize the Lies

*"Then you will know the truth, and
the truth will set you free."*

JOHN 8:32

"Dear Sharon," the letter began, "I found your e-mail on your website. I was searching for some information on what the Bible says about affairs. Somehow I came upon your site. I feel like I am on the verge of destroying my life. My life with my husband has never been good—marginal at best. I find myself working hard on my appearance so other men will notice and desire me. We have four children, and I'm miserable. My husband is in the military and away at boot camp. I'm glad he's gone.

"I am on the verge of having an affair with just about anyone to escape my marriage. I don't want to look back on my life and think I could have been happy with someone else. I feel like I am trapped in a loveless marriage. I want a divorce."

Can't you just see the enemy rubbing his hands together like an anxious fly? I bet he shuddered when she clicked the SEND button on her computer screen to send this e-mail to me. "Oh no," I imagine him saying. "This could ruin everything." He knew that I would help her recognize the lie.

Same Ol' Same Ol'

When you consider the words in the previous letter, they really aren't that different from the lies Eve believed in the Garden. *God is holding out on me...I would be happy if...I'm going to take control of this situation...Rain on the consequences. Anything is better than this.*

When I hear stories of women overcome with hopelessness and despair, my heart breaks. This is not what God had in mind when He sent His Son, Jesus Christ, to the earth to die on Calvary's Cross, rise from the darkened tomb, and ascend to heaven from the Mount. This is not what God intended for His bride when He gave her the gift and the power of the Holy Spirit. No, Jesus said, "I have come that they might have life, and have it to the full" (John 10:10). So what has happened to block the flow of abundant life into the hearts of men and women? Why are we not living in victory? Where is the living water? I believe the flow is blocked because we are believing lies rather than the truth.

Robert McGee, author of *Search for Significance,* wrote, "One of the biggest steps we can take toward consistently glorifying Christ and walking in peace and joy with our heavenly Father is to recognize the deceit which had held us captive. Satan's lies distort our true perspective, warp our thoughts, and produce painful emotions. If we cannot identify those lies, then it is very likely that we will continue to be defeated by them."[6]

John 10:10 reveals Jesus' intention for abundant life and the enemy's intention to block it. "The thief comes only to steal and kill and destroy; I have come that they might have life, and have it to the full." We have already realized who the real enemy is, and he is doing everything in his power to keep Christians from experiencing the abundant life. His ultimate goal is our utter destruction and his MO is lies.

The Bible says, "For we are not ignorant of his [Satan's] *schemes*" (2 Corinthians 2:11 NASB, emphasis added). "Put on the full armor of God so that you can take your stand against the devil's *schemes*" (Ephesians 6:11, emphasis added). His schemes include a step-by-step progressive plan of one lie that leads to another lie that leads to another lie. He begins small and works his way up to more destructive and disastrous misbeliefs. The way we stop the progression is to do as

Barney Fife suggests in *The Andy Griffith Show:* "Nip it in the bud." Recognize the lie the moment it enters your mind.

But the only way to recognize a lie is to know the truth. We must know the truth so that when a counterfeit comes along we recognize right away its lack of authenticity.

When someone is training to become a bank teller, he or she is taught how to recognize counterfeit money. However, the instructors do not teach what counterfeit bills look like. Rather, they teach what genuine money looks like. They study the markings, the coloring, and the feel of real money so when the counterfeit comes along, the teller can recognize it. D.L. Moody once said, "The best way to show that a stick is crooked is not to argue about it or to spend time denouncing it, but to lay a straight stick alongside it."[7]

Stinking Thinking

Martha was also frustrated with her marriage. She had dreams of marrying her knight in shining armor who would leave flower petals on her pillow, be distracted by her beauty, and regularly pledge his undying love. She dreamed of having three doting, obedient, well-mannered children that she could dress up in cute little outfits and parade down the church aisle on Sundays. Her tidy home would come with a well-manicured lawn, two and a half baths, and perfectly coordinated décor. She would be the happy homemaker who joyfully mopped the beautiful kitchen floor in her size six khaki slacks, shabby chic blouse, and stylish haircut. She could almost picture Mr. Clean winking at her from the corner of the room, giving his hearty approval.

But life had not turned out like Martha expected. Her knight did come along, but his armor began to tarnish soon after they said, "I do." He left his smelly socks on the floor, had a love affair with the TV remote, and hardly noticed all the work she did to keep the house clean and orderly.

Life sure has not turned out the way I thought it would, she thought. *I am bored and unappreciated. Romance, that's what I want. This man wouldn't know romance if it hit him in the face. Why should I care how I look? He doesn't care about his appearance. Look at that gut. He complains about me gaining weight? Well, he hasn't seen nothin' yet. I've made a huge mistake. I just want someone who will love me and appreciate me. Is that too much to ask?*

And the kids? They never do what I ask. They're disobedient, loud, and messy. I don't know when I've seen a clean floor last, and I'm sure not happy while mopping. And where is Mr. Clean anyway?

The enemy had slowly crept in while Martha was unaware. Unmet expectations became the breeding ground for the lies to grow. He planted the seeds of discontentment one disappointment at a time. Rather than thinking how she could make her marriage better, she began to think how she could get out of it. Rather than enjoying her rambunctious children, she loathed their energy. Rather than being thankful that she had a home and family to clean up after, she complained about the dirt.

"Martha just needs to give her life to Jesus," you might say. But she has. She is a Christian, so on top of her disappointment with life, she adds guilt to it all. *I'm a bad Christian,* she thinks. *If I were a better Christian, I'd be happy. What's wrong with me?*

The enemy's trademark is stamped on this woman's thought life. He has taken her down a road of stinkin' thinkin'. While she assumes that these thoughts are her own, it is the enemy who makes the suggestions. She simply buys into them and makes them her own. They become her own version of reality—her own version of the truth. But it is not God's truth. When we know the truth, the lies stick out like a two-ton elephant in a herd of sheep.

Truth-O-Meter

Paul gave us an effective lie detector to filter our thoughts through in Philippians 4:8-9.

> Finally, brothers, whatever is true, whatever is noble, whatever is right, whatever is pure, whatever is lovely, whatever is

admirable—if anything is excellent or praiseworthy—think about such things. Whatever you have learned or received or heard from me, or seen in me—put it into practice. And the God of peace will be with you.

Now that is a lot to think about. But the good news is we are not on our own. God has given us the power of the Holy Spirit to enable us to do all that He has called us to do.

Paul doesn't just leave us with the qualifying list; he gives us the means by which to implement it. "Whatever you have learned or received or heard from me, or seen in me—*put it into practice.*"

It takes practice. Practice, practice, *practice!*

But look at the result: "And the God of peace will be with you."

In this book, we are simply focusing on the very first command, "Whatever is true." If any thought begins with "what if," it is not true. It is worrying about something that has not happened. It is not reality. If any thought begins with "if only," it is not true. It is regret about something that has already happened that you can do nothing about. "Once we determine what is true and real," Elizabeth George says, "we can then function according to these facts instead of our feelings or fantasies."[8] Emotions are powerful. But if we want to walk in victory over our fickle feelings, we must first recognize the lies and replace the lies with truth.

Here's another idea. If you're not sure if a thought is from God or the enemy, attach "in Jesus' Name" to the end of it. For example:

"I just hate that woman, in Jesus' Name."

"I can't do this anymore, in Jesus' Name."

Hmmm. Something about that just doesn't fit, does it?

Pay Attention

Every weekday morning my husband's alarm clock goes off at 5:30. He gets up, showers, shaves, brushes his teeth, gets dressed, and places his jingling keys in his pocket. He clears his throat, blows his nose, and, well, does other noisy things. When he opens and closes the door

leading to the garage, the alarm in the bedroom beeps three times...
loudly. This happens every day, and I don't hear a thing. I sleep right
through it. My body has grown so accustomed to his routine that I
don't even hear the noise.

We can grow so accustomed to the lies, we don't even realize the
noise is there. The alarm may beep, but we ignore the alert. Our senses
grow dim.

David talked to himself regularly. In one psalm he wrote, "Awake,
my soul!" (Psalm 57:8). The Hebrew word translated "awake" could
be translated, "Pay attention! Open your eyes!"

We can get used to the lies and not even realize they are there. So
now it's time to wake up. Pay attention! Be on the alert! Watch out!
Don't be lulled into the hum of Satan's lies about who you are, what
you have, and where you are. "Awake, O my soul!" To win the war, we
must wake up to the battle and become *un*-desensitized to the lies.

Prepare for Take Off

Here we go again, I mused as the flight attendant began her routine
instructions. I grabbed the latest copy of *Sky Mall* magazine tucked
in the seat pocket in front of me and began flipping through the
pages. The man to my right continued reading the headlines in the
day's paper. The woman to my left was a first-time flyer and paid
close attention.

I glanced around the plane and noticed very few people listening to
the flight attendant's lifesaving instructions. And then it hit me. The
frequent flyers paid little attention, not because we were being rude,
but because we had heard it all before. The safety procedures were
routine information. The hum of the flight attendant's voice merged
with the whine of the engine. So we ignored her.

But you better believe that if the pilot announced mid-flight that
a crash landing was imminent, all of us "been there, done that" passengers would all be reviewing those safety instruction cards quicker
than you could say, "Buckle your seat belts."

Friend, we're getting ready to head into familiar territory for some.

I'll be reviewing safety instructions that you most likely have heard before. But I want you to read these truths from the Bible as if you are in danger of a crash landing. We never know when life will hit turbulence. Scrambling for the life jacket and fumbling with the oxygen mask on the way down is not the answer. We can be prepared so that when the storms hit, when the engines fail, when the machine runs out of gas, we'll be ready to land safely.

As you begin the process of detecting lies in your thought life, look objectively at any thoughts and attitudes that do not line up with Christ's teachings. When you recognize and expose the lie, you disarm its destructive potential in your life. Our power depends on believing the truth, and I pray that God will open our eyes to the power available to each and every one of us (Ephesians 1:18-19).

Buckle up. Let's get ready to fly.

- Realize the enemy's true identity.
- Recognize the lie.

4

Reject the Lies

*For though we live in the world, we do not wage
war as the world does. The weapons we fight with
are not weapons of the world. On the contrary, they
have divine power to demolish strongholds.*

2 CORINTHIANS 10:3-4

On July 16, 1999, John F. Kennedy Jr., his wife, Carolyn Bessette-Kennedy, and his sister-in-law, Lauren Bessette, met their death in a watery grave in the Atlantic Ocean. John was piloting the single-engine aircraft and was only a few miles from their destination when something went terribly wrong.

The plane left New Jersey en route to a family gathering in Massachusetts in the dark of night, and while crossing a thirty-mile stretch of water to make its final descent, the plane began a series of erratic maneuvers. John's descent varied between 400 and 800 feet per minute, about seven miles from shore. The plane began an erratic series of turns, descents, and climbs. Its final descent eventually exceeded 4700 fpm, and the airplane nose-dived into the ocean. The watery grave swallowed the plane and the three passengers on board.[9]

Other pilots flying similar routes on the night of the accident reported no visual horizon while flying over the water because of haze. They couldn't see a thing.

One pilot explained that John most likely experienced the "Black Hole" syndrome. Pilots of small-engine planes use the horizon as a reference point. However, John lost sight of the horizon and his eyes gave the brain no clue as to which way was up and which way was down. In this situation, if an airplane should turn slightly or nose down slightly, the body's inner ear compensates to make the pilot believe he's flying straight and level. If for some reason the pilot makes another correction, he can make a bad decision worse.

John was not flying under Instrument Flight Rules, but rather Visual Flight Rules. That means he was not trained to use the instrument panel properly, but simply learned how to fly by sight alone. When he could not see the horizon, John became disoriented and his mind lost its sense of perspective and direction. He had what we commonly call vertigo, and the flight pattern showed all the evidence of "mind wobbling and tortured confusion." John's instruments told him that his wings were tilted (flying sideways), but he *felt* that he was right-side up. While John had all the instruments on board for a safe landing, he did not know how to use them.

One pilot explained John's vertigo and disorientation this way: "And here is the crux of the matter; the pilot's emotions drowned out the flight instrument's story about banking and diving at high speed, and screamed out, 'No way! It can't be. I'm actually flying straight and level. I know it!'" [10]

A skilled instrument flyer knows he can't rely on his feelings and has the ability to regain control of the airplane by depending on the instruments. Instructors call this lifesaving skill "recovery from unusual attitudes." "The real skill of instrument flying is truly depending on the instrument's readings rather than your feelings. Recovery from 'unusual attitudes' consists of one essential belief: your feelings cannot be trusted as the final authority on what the airplane is doing. Your mind is boss. The instruments are your window on reality and you desperately need to understand the data they provide." [11]

Friend, I hope you are tracking with me. This isn't just about flying an airplane; this is about maneuvering through life. John had everything he needed to make a safe landing right there on the instrument panel in front of him. But he didn't know how to use them. John chose to rely on his feelings rather than the facts. His feelings lied, and he and his passengers died.

We have the opportunity to learn how to fly through the storms of life with limited visibility. We can maneuver safely through unexpected turbulence and relational malfunctions. God has given us the tools to avoid becoming disoriented and going into a tailspin or nosedive. His Word is the Truth that guides us through the inky soup when the horizon is nowhere in sight. His Word *is* the instrument panel. However, if we rely on our feelings we won't know which way is up and which way is down.

The Shield of Faith

We are in a spiritual battle for our minds. And while we often think difficult people or circumstances are the source of the problems in our lives, Paul tells us to look past the obvious and go to the root cause. "For our struggle is not against flesh and blood," Paul begins, "but against the rulers, against the authorities, against the powers of this dark world and against the spiritual forces of evil in the heavenly realms" (Ephesians 6:12). As long as we think our foe is a mere mortal, the enemy is sittin' pretty. But we've already realized the enemy's true identity. Right?

This spiritual battle is described as a "struggle." It literally means "wrestling" or "hand-to-hand" combat.[12] In other places in the New Testament, Paul refers to the spiritual battle we face every day. He told Timothy to "fight the good fight of the faith" (1 Timothy 6:12). And he said of himself, "I have fought the good fight, I have finished the race, I have kept the faith" (2 Timothy 4:7). He encourages Timothy to endure hardship as a "good soldier of Christ Jesus" (2 Timothy 2:3).

Yes, Jesus won the victory over sin and death when He died on the cross and rose again. Satan was defeated. However, until we leave this earth and the presence of sin, we continue to fight against the power of sin and the lies that hold us back.

This warfare is nothing to fear. God has given us sufficient armor to combat the enemy's schemes. We have the power of the Holy Spirit working in us, the power of Jesus' shed blood over us, and the power of God's Word under our feet. Let's take a look at the armor Paul instructs us to wear in this battle for the truth.

> Therefore put on the full armor of God, so that when the day of evil comes, you may be able to stand your ground, and after you have done everything, to stand. Stand firm then, with the belt of truth buckled around your waist, with the breastplate of righteousness in place, and with your feet fitted with the readiness that comes from the gospel of peace. In addition to all this, take up the shield of faith, with which you can extinguish all the flaming arrows of the evil one. Take the helmet of salvation and the sword of the Spirit, which is the word of God (Ephesians 6:13-17).

While Paul tells us to take up the *full* armor of God, the *shield of faith* has captured my attention here. The belt, breastplate, and sandals or boots were worn continually in battle, but the helmet, sword, and shield were worn only when the fighting began. When speaking of the shield, Paul is describing a large Roman shield covered with leather, which could be soaked in water and used to put out flame-tipped arrows.[13] As Satan shoots his fiery lies, we hold up our shield of faith (what we know to be true) to block the lies and extinguish their flames.

And we must block them right away. For example, Satan whispers the thought into my head, *I'm so stupid.* As soon as the thought comes knocking at the door of my mind, I can do one of two things. I can believe the lie or I can reject the lie by saying, "That's not true. That is a lie of the enemy. I made a mistake, but I have the mind of Christ."

We cannot act differently than we believe. That is why it is so important to reject the lie as soon as it comes.

There are certain television jingles that drive my husband crazy. As soon as he sees a nanosecond of commercial appear, he presses the mute button. And while I tease him for being a commercial phobic, you know what happens to me? I end up with that silly song in my head for the rest of the evening. He has the right idea—mute it, delete it, don't give it a chance to enter your mind.

The thief comes to steal, kill, and destroy, and he does it one thought at a time. The thoughts are not your thoughts and don't become your thoughts until you allow them to cross the threshold of the mind. Once you embrace the lie as your own, and begin telling yourself the lie, it begins to do its damage. As God said to Cain, "Sin is crouching at your door; it desires to have you, but you must master it" (Genesis 4:7).

I love what David prayed in Psalm 119:29-30: "Keep me from deceitful ways...I have chosen the way of truth." Perhaps "keep me from deceitful ways" is a wonderful prayer to start the morning, and "I have chosen the way of truth" a perfect bookend at day's end.

The Nature of Faith

So what is faith? Hebrews 11:1 gives us a wonderful definition: "Now faith is being sure of what we hope for and certain of what we do not see." Another translation expounds on that same verse: "Now faith is the assurance (the confirmation, the title deed) of things [we] hope for, being the proof of things [we] do not see and the conviction of their reality [faith perceiving as real fact what is not revealed to the senses]" (AMP). It is that trust in God that enables believers to press on whatever the future holds for them. They know they can rely on God. Holding up the shield of faith is holding up what you know to be true from God's Word.

Faith is simply this—believing God. It is acting as though God tells the truth. "Abram believed the LORD, and he credited it to him as righteousness" (Genesis 15:6). He believed in the promises of God regardless of what his emotions told him. I'm sure as the years passed by and Abraham became an old man, Satan tempted him to doubt God's promise that he would be the father of many nations. However, he held up his shield of faith, extinguished the darts of doubt, and continued to believe.

The Stance of Faith

Notice how many times Paul admonishes us to *stand* in Ephesians 6. "Therefore put on the full armor of God, so that when the day of evil comes, you may be able to *stand* your ground, and after you have done everything, to *stand*. *Stand* firm then…" No one can stand for us. We have to stand on our own two feet and stand up against the enemy—and we stand on the Word of Truth.

Being from North Carolina, I love the old black-and-white Andy Griffith television programs. In one episode, the neighborhood bully is picking on Opie. This blond-headed newcomer taunts and makes fun of Opie until he feels as if he's a total loser among the buddies he once enjoyed. After Andy, the wise father, figures out what is disturbing his moping son, he gives him a little lesson in standing up to bullies. The next day, when the bully threatens Opie, the little freckle-faced boy looks his opponent in the eye and refuses to crumble under his threats.

"Do you want to fight?" the bully taunts.

Opie doesn't say a word, just puts up his fists.

"Oh yeah, well knock this rock off my shoulder and I'll—"

Opie knocks the rock off his shoulder before the bully has time to finish his sentence.

"Oh yeah, well step into this circle," the bully continues as he draws a circle around himself in the dirt.

Opie steps into the circle.

Suddenly, the bully grows nervous. "You better be glad I've got on my good pants," the bully says as he backs away.

Opie never had to throw the first punch. All he did was stand his ground and the enemy backed away. Bullies don't like it when we stand up to them. Never have. Never will.

The Lord said through the prophet Isaiah, "If you do not *stand* firm in your faith, you will not *stand* at all" (Isaiah 7:9). As the old song-writer penned, "On Christ the solid Rock I *stand,* all other ground is sinking sand."

"Now it is God who makes both us and you *stand firm* in Christ,"

Paul wrote. "He anointed us, set his seal of ownership on us, and put his Spirit in our hearts as a deposit, guaranteeing what is to come" (2 Corinthians 1:21-22). And David said,

> He lifted me out of the slimy pit,
>   out of the mud and mire;
> he set my feet on a rock
>   and gave me a *firm place to stand*
>   (Psalm 40:2).

Maybe you've been running from the bully for way too long. He's all bark and no bite. He's a toothless cowardly lion. Go ahead. Take your stand.

The Power of Faith

Just as Paul wrote to the Ephesians about the spiritual warfare we face on a daily basis, he also wrote to the Corinthians:

> For though we live in the world, we do not wage war as the world does. The weapons we fight with are not the weapons of the world. On the contrary, they have divine power to demolish strongholds. We demolish arguments and every pretension that sets itself up against the knowledge of God, and we take captive every thought to make it obedient to Christ (2 Corinthians 10:3-5).

What exactly is a stronghold? A stronghold is a thought pattern that forms a fortress around the mind, holding it prisoner to faulty thinking. It is formed brick by brick by repetitive faulty thinking or all at once by a onetime traumatic event such as a rape, molestation, or abuse.

In the Old Testament, a stronghold was a fortified dwelling used for protection from an enemy. David hid in wilderness strongholds when he was hiding from King Saul, who was trying to kill him (1 Samuel 22:4; 23:14). These were usually caves high on a mountainside or some other structure that was hard to attack. In the Old

Testament, God is called our stronghold: "The LORD is a refuge for the oppressed, a stronghold in times of trouble" (Psalm 9:9).

The New Testament writers took this same imagery of a fortress to describe the spiritual tower of bondage, not protection, that we put ourselves in by developing thought patterns and ideas that hold us captive. Beth Moore calls a stronghold, "Anything that we hold onto that ends up holding onto us." It is anything that sets itself up against the knowledge of God. A stronghold does not protect us, it protects the enemy who is manipulating our thoughts and suggesting our actions.

The only way to expose the enemy and defeat him is to tear down the stronghold, the fortress where he is hiding. An ungodly habit becomes his habitation, his stronghold in our lives. Once you recognize a lie in your life—perhaps something that has even taken hold of your imagination and stirred ungodly feelings such as jealousy, worry, fear, or anger—you reject the lie and replace it with truth. Each time you reject a lie, you knock one more brick from the enemy's fortress, and pretty soon, he's exposed for the liar and deceiver he is.

I do not want to give the impression that this is an easy process. Some of us are so comfortable with our strongholds we don't even realize they are there. That was the case with me. I had been walking around saved but enslaved for so many years. I drug the ball and chain of inferiority, insecurity, and inadequacy around with me everywhere I went, and I grew so used to my limp, I didn't even notice it. I was comfortable with my weakness and served Satan a cup of tea every day I sat hidden away behind the wall he had helped me build. But praise God, Jesus opened my eyes to the truth and called me out of the fortress that had become my prison cell. I got distracted by holy excitement over what God has done.

Let's go back to the idea that destroying strongholds is not easy. It's simple, but not easy. Paul used words such as *struggle, resist, tear down,* and *fight.* The good news is that we're not a one-woman demolition crew. The Holy Spirit gives us the power, Jesus gives us the light, and God is overseeing the entire project. We simply agree to participate through obedience.

When we talk about strongholds, we're not talking about random thoughts or occasional sins. A stronghold is a thought pattern or habitual sin. It is a fortress built with the bricks of thoughts and held together by the mortar of emotions. Strongholds become our perception of reality.

In my own life, replacing self-defeating lies with God's truth chipped away at the stronghold of inadequacy that led to a negative cycle of discouragement, despair, and defeat. Rejecting the lie will tear down those strongholds, and after a time, even the ruins are removed.

In addition to strongholds, we demolish arguments and every pretension that sets itself up against the knowledge of God. "Thoughts, ideas, speculations, reasonings, philosophies, and false religions are the ideological forts in which people barricade themselves against God and the gospel," John MacArthur says.[14] Paul fought vehemently against false prophets or anyone who dared add or subtract from the pure message of the gospel.

Just as Dorothy's little dog, Toto, exposed the great wizard in *The Wizard of Oz,* when we realize the enemy's true identity, recognize the lie, and pull the curtain back to reject the lie, we'll find a washed-up old phony who relies on deceptive maneuvers, bells, and whistles to keep his subjects trembling in fear.

I just love when Dorothy looks at the "the great wizard" and says, "Why you're just an old man." He'd been found out by a farm girl and her little dog.

The New American Standard Bible says that we are "destroying speculations and every lofty thing raised up against the knowledge of God." Those words sound ominous and grand: *speculations…lofty thing.* But speculation could be something as simple as falling into the trap of worrying about the future. *What if my husband loses his job? What if my child gets sick and dies? What if I get cancer? What if my children don't follow Christ when they grow up? What if my husband leaves me? What if, what if, what if…*

Worry is no more than speculation about the future that will rob you of joy in the present. It is not thinking on what is real or true.

Those thoughts must be taken captive to the obedience of Christ. Reject the lies. Hold up the shield of faith. Stand firm in the truth.

Swollen Imaginations

Ada had an uneventful dental visit at my husband's office—just a routine filling. He was surprised when she called him at home later that evening, complaining of a swollen cheek and excruciating pain.

"Dr. Jaynes," she groaned, "I can barely hold my head up. My face is swollen, I can't open my mouth, and the pain is severe."

"Ada, I'm so sorry you're having trouble," Steve said. "I can't imagine what the problem could be. I'll call you in some pain medicine and you come in first thing in the morning."

The following day, I was working as Steve's assistant and was amazed at Ada's appearance when she arrived at the office. Her eyes were half closed, she could barely walk, and her right cheek did appear quite swollen. Ada sat down in the chair as if every movement took great effort. She could barely open her mouth to let Steve see what the problem might be. Finally, she did manage to open slightly. Steve gently lifted her lip, and a huge grin spread across his face. He reached in with an instrument and removed a cotton roll from between her cheek and tooth.

Ada's eyes popped open as she bolted upright in the chair. "What did you do?" she exclaimed, all signs of weakness gone. Ada was miraculously healed.

Steve grinned and held up the small piece of cotton. "This is what was causing you so much 'pain.'"

Ada was terribly embarrassed.

Steve and I replayed the scenes from the previous day. Before placing the filling, he put a small cotton roll between Ada's cheek and tooth to keep the area dry. I was assisting him that day and forgot to remove the cotton roll when he had finished. When the anesthesia wore off, Ada felt her cheek and thought it was swollen. As the night wore on, her imagination ran rampant until she had worked herself into such a state, she could barely move. She had made herself sick.

Never once did she open her mouth and look inside. If she had, she would have seen a little white piece of cotton.[15]

That is the power of our imagination and faulty thinking. We can talk ourselves into believing a lie to the point that it affects our actions and our emotions and even our health. But with close examination, we can recognize the lie and stand on the truth.

Finally, Paul writes to "take every thought captive to make it obedient to Christ." Just like the policeman who pursues and captures a criminal on the loose, we can capture those runaway thoughts and lock them away for good. Oh, Satan will try to post bail and set them loose again. But we have the power and the authority to lock them up and throw away the key.

Rosa Rejects the Lie

Rosa stood in line for nearly an hour waiting for everyone to clear away. She was a beautiful Latino woman who attended a conference where I spoke in Mexico City. With the help of an interpreter, Rosa poured out her heart. When she was in her twenties, she married and had two small children. Her husband was not pleased when she discovered that she was pregnant with their third child. "You cannot have another baby," he said. "You must have an abortion or I'm going to leave you."

Rosa was torn. Like her husband, she did not want this baby. Her marriage was in shambles, their finances were in a mess, and she was exhausted trying to keep up with the two little ones she already had. However, her religious convictions told her that abortion was wrong. The fear of living without her husband's support drove Rosa to the abortion clinic. But before the procedure began, she changed her mind and ran from the building.

"I did not have the abortion," Rosa said with tears in her eyes, "but I wanted to. My daughter is now twenty-one years old and has been the joy of my life. Of all my children, she treats me the best. But I have carried this guilt around with me for all these years. How could I have considered aborting her? What kind of person am I?"

Rosa broke down in sobs as I and the interpreter tried to comfort her. She had asked God to forgive her, and truly believed that He had. But she could not forgive herself. For twenty-one years, Satan whispered a lie into her heart: "This is the child you didn't want. This is the child you almost killed. What kind of person are you?"

Rosa had believed the lie, but on this day in July 2007, she learned to hold up her shield of faith and extinguish the fiery arrows.

"Rosa, do you believe that God forgave you?"

"Yes."

"Rosa, do you believe that what Jesus did for you on the cross was enough to pay for the penalty of your sins?"

"Yes."

"Do you believe 1 John 1:9 that says if you confess your sins, God is faithful and just and will forgive your sins and purify you from all unrighteousness?"

"Yes."

"Sister, you are forgiven. It is the enemy who is lying to you and whispering words of shame and condemnation. He is the accuser, but God has already stamped 'Not guilty' on your heart. Jesus came to set you free. Don't hold out your hands for Satan to slap on those handcuffs of guilt and condemnation any longer."

Rosa chose to begin rejecting the lie. She held up her shield of faith that day...and the next...and the next...and the next. C.S. Lewis wrote, "Relying on God has to begin all over again every day as if nothing yet had been done."[16] Rosa discovered that freedom is just a truth away.

The Peace of the Truth

We began this chapter in an airplane, but let me take you to another ride—not across the sky but down the treacherous, snake-infested Amazon River.

Steve and I sat anxiously in our seats. I wondered if I was going to be able to endure the ride, especially knowing my propensity for motion sickness. But we began nonetheless.

The guide strapped all passengers into the tiny boats and gave last minute instructions. Of course there were life preservers, but what good would they do in the fierce rapids that threatened to suck its prey below the surface?

The crew boarded and began the journey down the mysterious Amazon. The calm meandering waters quickly gave way to fierce torrents, rushing rapids, and rocky crags protruding from the foaming waters. Alternating between plunging into the water and flying into the air, the boat made its way through the first set of rapids. My body relaxed, thankful that was over. Several times along the journey calm gave way to chaos as passengers maneuvered to keep the boats afloat. Often, I closed my eyes and waited for the turbulence to pass.

When we finally reached the end of our journey, I picked up my popcorn and walked out of the theater.

No, I wasn't really on the Amazon River strapped in a tiny boat. I was comfortably sitting in a cushioned chair in the IMAX theater watching a documentary about the Amazon River. In the five-story domed screen covering 6532 square feet of projection surface, large images put you in the center of the action, and the surround sound gave the illusion that you were indeed wherever the screen took you. It wasn't real.

Yes, I did get a bit queasy from the larger-than-life movement down the river, but I was never in real danger. Even though the producers and engineer tried their best to create a realistic experience, I knew it wasn't true. It was a movie. I would walk out unscathed.

That is the peace of walking, or in this case sitting, in the truth.

- Realize the enemy's true identity.
- Recognize the lie.
- Reject the lie.

5

Replace the Lies with Truth

Finally brothers and sisters, whatever
is true...think about such things.

Philippians 4:8

For fifteen years, Leeanne was emotionally and verbally abused by her mother. Every day she heard that she was a stupid worthless failure. Her mother told her that she was "ugly" and "fat" and "not good enough." "No man will ever want you," she said.

Leeanne grew up afraid of women and hating herself. "Why can't I be different?" she wondered. She believed her mother's estimation of her and lived in defeat. Leeanne grabbed attention any way she could, and by the time she was twenty-three, she had three abortions on her medical record. The guilt and shame of those abortions compounded her feelings of worthlessness.

But something amazing happened to Leeanne when she was twenty-four. She accepted Jesus as her Lord and Savior and became a new creation. She knew that God forgave her the moment she asked—totally and completely. However, Satan continued to remind her of the terrible mistakes of her past. *How could I have killed my children? What would my friends think if they knew the truth? I can never let anyone know about my past. Some things are simply unforgivable in human eyes.*

Leeanne met and married a wonderful Christian man. They began their life of ministry as he pastored a church in a small community. God blessed them with three wonderful children, but still the shame of her past lingered.

"I felt so unworthy of my husband's love," she said. "I felt I wasn't good enough to be his wife. I never told him about my past. It was a secret that weighed me down."

Leeanne went to a women's retreat and picked up one of my books, *Your Scars Are Beautiful to God.* For the first time, she began to heal from the wounds her mother had inflicted on her little-girl heart. She realized that it was Satan who continued to taunt her with those lies and make her feel as if they were true. Then she did something that really made the enemy mad. She forgave her mother. Even though her mother had since died, she forgave her as if she were standing before her that very day.

Leeanne imagined Jesus erasing away all her faults, especially the ones her mother had so maliciously written on the chalkboard of her mind. "All gone," she said. "I'm set free."

But there was one more step to Leeanne's freedom. As long as she kept her past a secret, she would never be totally free.

"I prayed all day and night for the courage to tell my husband about the three abortions. No one in the world knew about the abortions but me. I had to tell my husband the secret so Satan could not use it against me any longer.

"Finally, I did it. I told him the truth. But he did not react the way I imagined he would. He held me in his arms and cried. 'I can't believe you have held on to this for so long alone,' he said. He was amazing.

"I am no longer shameful. I am pure.

"I am no longer ugly. I am beautiful.

"I am no longer unlovable. I am dearly loved."

Leeanne recognized the lies. Leeanne rejected the lies. Leeanne replaced the lies with truth. She is now walking in the truth as a holy, chosen, dearly loved child of God.

Learning from the Best

In chapter two we looked at how Eve lost her battle with the enemy in the Garden. Now let's take a look at how Jesus won the battle with that same enemy in the desert. It all began with His baptism.

"Repent and be baptized!" the prophet called to those gathered around the Jordan River. People from all around Jerusalem and Judea came to hear this man called John preach about forgiveness and repentance of sins. They wondered if he could be the Messiah, but John assured them he was not. "I baptize you with water," he said. "But one more powerful than I will come, the thongs of whose sandals I am not worthy to untie" (Luke 3:16).

One day John saw Jesus emerge from the crowd. John held out his arms and proclaimed, "Look, the Lamb of God, who takes away the sin of the world!"

Jesus presented himself for baptism, and as he came up from the water, the clouds parted, a dove descended, and God spoke: "You are my Son, whom I love; with you I am well pleased" (Luke 3:22).

It was a red-letter day on the kingdom calendar when the culmination of God's incredible plan of redemption was set into motion. And where was Jesus' first assignment? It was in the desert, face-to-face with his nemesis—the enemy He came to destroy.

For forty days and nights Jesus went without food and water and was tempted by the devil in the wilderness.

"If you are the Son of God, tell these stones to become bread," Satan said.

"It is written: 'Man does not live on bread alone, but on every word that comes from the mouth of God.'" Jesus pulled out the Sword of the Spirit—the Word of God—and plunged it into Satan's lie.

Once again the enemy taunted Him and took Him to the highest point of the temple. "If you are the Son of God, throw yourself down. For it is written: 'He will command his angels concerning you, and they will lift you up in their hands, so that you will not strike your foot against a stone.'"

Once again, Jesus fought back with the truth: "It is also written: 'Do not put the Lord your God to the test.'"

Again, the devil took Jesus to a very high mountain and showed him all the kingdoms of the world and their splendor. "All this I will give you," he said, "if you will bow down and worship me."

Again, Jesus wielded his sword. "Away from me, Satan! For it is written: 'Worship the Lord your God, and serve him only.'"

Defeated, Satan tucked his tail and slunk away...to wait for a more opportune time (Luke 4:13). Yes, he left Jesus alone that day, but he declared, *I'll be back.* And come back he did.

Jesus won the battle in the wilderness by standing firm on the truth. Oh dear one, how foolish we are to think the garden is where our lives will be trouble free. It is not our circumstances that determine a life of joy and victory. Jesus experienced victory in the desert. Eve experienced defeat in comfort and ease.

Singing a New Song

Lies can become a haunting hum in your head, like a song you just can't shake. And the best way to get the annoying tune out of your mind is to replace it with a new one. As King David wrote, "He put a new song in my mouth" (Psalm 40:3).

As we've already seen, there is a battle going on for our thought life, and this is where the fighting heats up. We've realized the enemy's true identity, recognized the lies, and rejected the lies. Now it's time to pull out the sword, the Word of God, and cut the enemy down to size. Jesus didn't win the battle by outsmarting the devil. He won the war by out truthing him. If it worked for Jesus, it will work for us.

One of the primary messages of the book of John is truth. It is one of the most repeated words spoken by Jesus and the most recorded word in John's gospel—seventy-seven times in the New International Version. To cite a few examples:

- "But whoever lives by the *truth* comes into the light, so that it may be seen plainly that what he has done has been done through God" (John 3:21).

- Jesus answered, "I am the way and the *truth* and the life. No one comes to the Father except through me" (John 14:6).

- Jesus prayed, "Sanctify them by the *truth;* your word is truth" (John 17:17).

More than seventy times in the Gospel of John, Jesus began his statements with "I tell you the truth." Why? I believe He was trying to get our attention, to emphasize His point, and to let us know He is trustworthy. He wants us not only to believe *in* Him, but to believe Him.

Discovering the Truth

John begins his account of the gospel, "In the beginning was the Word, and the Word was with God, and the Word was God. He was with God in the beginning" (John 1:1). The Greek word for Word is *logos* and refers to the entire expression of God revealed to man. It is the direct revelation of God to man.

There is another Greek word that is translated "word"—*rhema*. As *logos* is the entire Word of God, *rhema* is a particular passage of Scripture that God quickens to your spirit. As we store up the *logos* of God in our hearts, God will open our eyes to understand a personal *rhema*. This may occur when you're reading the Bible or when the Holy Spirit brings a verse to mind that you have previously read.

Two people can be reading the same passage of Scripture. One may see something that speaks to her about a specific situation she's experiencing in her life while the other moves along unaffected. This happens often with my husband and me as we're reading the Bible or listening to a sermon together. I get all excited and shout, "Man, did you hear that? Did you see that?" Steve just looks at me and says, "Sure, honey." Then I know that I had just experienced a *rhema* from God specifically for me. At other times, Steve gets out his marker and with a gleam in his eye highlights a passage meant just for him. God is very personal and intimate with each of His children and has specific revelations for anyone who takes the time to study His Word.

Now, let's go back to Paul's letter to the Ephesians, specifically focusing on the armor of God in chapter six. We've already looked at the shield of faith and how we are to resist and reject the lies of the enemy. Now let's pull out the sword of the Spirit and chase him off for good.

Paul writes: "Take the helmet of salvation and the sword of the Spirit, which is the word of God" (Ephesians 6:17). Guess which Greek word is used for "word"? *Rhema*—a *particular* word that the Holy Spirit brings to our remembrance. But remember, in order for the Holy Spirit to bring a *rhema* to our remembrance, the *logos* has to be deposited in our memory banks first.

You can read the Bible (*logos*) and still not experience the power of God in your life. Jesus challenged the religious leaders, "You diligently study the Scriptures because you think that by them you possess eternal life. These are the Scriptures that testify about me, yet you refuse to come to me to have life" (John 5:39-40). The Holy Spirit dwelling in the believer's heart shines the understanding light of Christ on the written words and transforms them into *rhema* words from God.

Reprogramming the Mind

When God created man, He created us in three parts: body, soul, and spirit. The earthly body is the part we see and houses the five senses. It is temporary and lasts for only a short time, though it will be transformed at the resurrection. The spirit is the inner man that communicates with God and lives for eternity. This is the part of us that is "born again" when we come to Christ.

The third part of man, the soul, is what makes up our personality. It is made up of three parts: mind, will, emotions. We receive information into our minds, we act on that information with our will, and we feel a response with our emotions. The brain is part of the body and is different from the mind. The mind actually uses the brain just as we use a computer to store, enter, and search for information.

Now that the spiritual anatomy lesson is over, let's see how that applies to overcoming the lies women tell themselves. From the day we are born physically to the day we are born again spiritually, we develop habit patterns and thought patterns to get our God-given needs of safety, security, and significance met apart from God. These thought patterns are stored in our minds, on the hard drive, and become the operating system that our actions and emotions depend on for direction. The input for the computer comes from the messages we receive and how we interpret the data.

When we become a new creation in Christ, no one pushes the delete button to remove the old ways of thinking; rather we must participate with God to reprogram the computer, the mind. Paul teaches, "Do not be conformed to this world, but be transformed by the renewing of your mind" (Romans 12:1). As we begin to recognize the lies, reject the lies, and replace the lies with truth, we will be renewing our minds to think biblically and truthfully.

On my patio I have a fountain attached to the wall. Often it gets filled with leaves and other debris. Since I cannot remove it from the wall to dump out the trash, I had to come up with another way to clean it out. I simply put a hose in the fountain and fill it to overflowing with clean water. As the clean water fills the fountain, the debris-filled water spills over the edge. The clean water flows in and displaces the dirty water until it is crystal clear once again.

That's what happens as we fill our minds with the truth. It displaces and replaces the lies.

In our own lives, as we begin to replace the lies with truth, the pure water of God's Word will begin to displace the muck and mire in our minds. I've often longed for a plug to pull so all the old thought patterns could be removed quickly and easily. But more often than not, God uses a truth to replace the lie rather than simply removing the lie and leaving an empty space.

Bible teacher Beth Moore compares renewing your mind to replacing wallpaper. I just finished taking down the wallpaper in my guest bathroom. It was a difficult and time-consuming task. I scored the paper with a sharp instrument, wiped down the wall with a stripping solution, and attempted to peel the old paper from the wall. I'd get so excited when I removed a large piece, but most of the time it was pick, pick, pick. With my fingernails and a putty knife, I removed bits at a time until all the old wallpaper was gone.

I wish I could tell you that re-wallpapering your mind is easy, but it's not. Oh sure, sometimes you get a big piece to come off all at once.

There are times when a great mental and spiritual victory pulls down a big chunk of that old thinking. But most of the time it is a tedious process that takes patience, determination, and spiritual stamina. But the end result is an amazing peace.

Psychiatrist Paul Meier conducted a study on the effect of meditation among seminary students. He concluded, "Daily meditation on Scripture, with personal application, is the most effective means of obtaining personal joy, peace, and emotional maturity...On average, it takes about three years of daily Scripture meditation to bring about enough change in a person's thought patterns and behavior to produce statistically superior mental health and happiness."[17]

Seeing Yourself as God Sees You

If you have believed the lies about who you are, it might take some time to begin seeing yourself as God sees you. Sometimes we are hesitant to embrace the truth about who we are as a child of God: holy, chosen, redeemed, and dearly loved. We find it easier to believe the lies, because they are what we've heard all our lives.

I remember sitting with my country grandmother in the summer of 1969 watching Neil Armstrong walk on the moon. "That's a bunch of hogwash," Grandma spat. "There's no way that man is really on the moon. He's just walking around on some television set. I'll never believe that's real. How stupid do those people think we are anyway?"

Well, Grandma, it was real. Apollo 11 landed on the moon and Mr. Armstrong took a stroll. Not only that, but it was only the beginning of several human footprints that marked the dusty lunar surface in years to come.

But the truth was just too farfetched for Grandma. She never believed it. Some think who they are in Christ is too far-fetched to believe. But when they refuse, they miss a tremendous blessing.

The way you think about yourself will become the way you see yourself, whether it's true or false. Eventually, you'll believe what you tell yourself. If you tell yourself negative, distorted statements about yourself, you will act in negative, destructive ways. If you replace the lies with the truth about who you really are, then you will begin to walk, talk, and live like the child of God you are.

Your beliefs will affect your behavior. You cannot act differently than what you believe. That's why we're starting at the top...we're starting with the mind, the thought life.

So what about you? I'm not talking about the moon now, I'm talking about the Son. Will you believe the truth about who you are, what you have, and where you are as a child of God? Will you begin to reject the lies and stand on the truth? Will you begin to see yourself as God sees you? Oh, I hope the answers to those questions were *yes*. They were for Suzanne.

Changing "I Can't" to "I Can"

Suzanne had been severely depressed and anxious for months. In desperation, she checked into a hospital for treatment. Medication seemed only to make her thinking cloudy, and she was having a difficult time focusing. It was hard to even remember which medication to take, and she often found herself crying for hours at a time. "I can't do anything right," she cried. "I can't even remember which medication to take when."

Her sister e-mailed her a devotion I had written about replacing lies with the truth. Suzanne knew that she would not be able to concentrate long enough to read the entire devotion, so she printed it off to read a little at a time. When she started reading, she couldn't put it down. In the devotion, I made a simple suggestion: "If you find yourself saying, 'I can't do anything right,' stop right there and ask if that thought is from God."

Suzanne knew that God was about to tell her something significant. Given the circumstances of the last month in the psychiatric hospital and the new drugs she was on, she was having a difficult time doing anything correctly. She read on...

"If you aren't sure if a thought is the truth or a lie, try this simple test. Add 'in Jesus' Name' to the end of it. For example: "I can't do anything right, in Jesus' Name.' Hmmm. That just doesn't seem to fit does it? How about, 'I'm a loser, in Jesus' Name.' Nope that doesn't fit either.

"Now, when you recognize that you are telling yourself a lie, stop and replace it with the truth."

Suzanne decided she would give it a try. She recognized that she had been believing lies of the enemy rather than the truth of God. It made so much sense to her. She kept repeating the phrase, "I can't do anything right, in Jesus' Name," and finally understood this thought could not be from God. With this realization, she felt the darkness start to lift and decided she needed to try something simple that she could accomplish.

"I'll sew a seam," she thought. She sewed the seam, and then turned it over to discover that she had missed an area. But rather than saying the usual, "I can't do anything right," she laughed at herself. Laughed for the first time in weeks. Then she said, "I'm going to try this again because I can do something right, in Jesus' Name." And she did it.

The writer of Proverbs states, "As [a man] thinks within himself, so he is" (Proverbs 23:7 NASB). Suzanne began seeing herself as God saw her, and it changed the way she saw herself.

Here's an added bonus to the story. Suzanne had felt that God had given up on her, but when her sister's e-mail came at her very point of need, she knew that God still loved her dearly and hadn't given up on her at all. He was right there prompting her sister to send her the very message she needed to hear.

Don't you just love God!

Part 2

The Lies Women
Tell Themselves

6

I'm Not Good Enough

LIE: *I'm not good enough.*

TRUTH: *I am good enough because Christ dwells in me and the Holy Spirit empowers me (John 14:20; Acts 1:8).*

Anabel Gillham loved God, but she had trouble accepting that God could love her. Sure, she knew the Bible verses that talked of God's unconditional love for her. And yet she knew herself and doubted that a God who knew her innermost thoughts would approve of her.

The root of her problem was how she saw God and how she believed God saw her. She knew what kind of God He was. She read Exodus 34:6, "And [the LORD] passed in front of Moses, proclaiming, 'The LORD, the LORD, the compassionate and gracious God, slow to anger, abounding in love and faithfulness, maintaining love to thousands, and forgiving wickedness, rebellion and sin.'" But she believed she had to earn that love. She believed she had to be good enough to deserve it. Then God used a very special person to help Annabel understand the depths of God's love for her—her second child, Mason David Gillham, who was profoundly retarded. I'll let Anabel tell you her story.

> Mace could sing one song with great gusto, just one: "Jesus Loves Me." He would throw his head back and hold on to the first "Yes" in the chorus just as long as he could, and then he would get tickled and almost fall out of his chair. I can still hear him giggle when I think back on those days that seem so distant and so far away. How poignant that memory is to me.

I never doubted for a moment that Jesus loved that profoundly retarded little boy. It didn't matter that he would never sit with the kids in the back of the church and on a certain special night walk down the aisle, take the pastor by the hand, and invite Jesus into his heart. It was entirely irrelevant that he could not quote a single verse of Scripture, that he would never go to high school, or that he would never be a dad. I knew that Jesus loved Mason.

What I could not comprehend, what I could not accept, was that Jesus could love Mason's mother, Anabel. You see, I believed that in order for a person to accept me, to love me, I had to perform for him. My standard for getting love was performance-based, so I "performed" constantly, perfectly. In fact, I did not allow anyone to see me when I was not performing perfectly. I never had any close friends because I was convinced that if a person ever really got to know me, he wouldn't like me.

I carried this belief into my relationship with God, and, as I began to study the Bible, I found, to my horror, that He knew my every thought, let alone everything I said or did (Psalm 139:1- 4). I was standing "bare and wide open to the all-seeing eyes of our living God" (Hebrews 4:13 TLB). What did that mean to me? That meant that He really knew me, that He saw me when I wasn't performing well. Based on what I perceived as my responsibility to perform in order to receive acceptance, I concluded without a doubt that He could not possibly love me, that He could never like what He saw.

Mace could never have performed for our love, or for anyone's love, but oh, how we loved him. His condition deteriorated to such a degree—and so rapidly—that we had to institutional- ize him when he was very young, so we enrolled him in the Enid State School for Mentally Handicapped Children. We drove regularly the 120 miles to see him, but on this particular weekend, he was at home for a visit. He had been with us since Thursday evening, and it was now Saturday afternoon. As soon as the dinner dishes were done, I would gather his things together and take him back to *his* house. I had done this many times before—and it was never easy—but today God had something in mind that would change my life forever.

As I was washing the dishes, Mason was sitting in his chair watching me, or at least he was looking at me. That's when it began. My emotions were spinning, my stomach started tumbling, and the familiar sickening thoughts of just a little while, I'm going to start packing Mason's toys and his clothes and take him away again. I can't do that. I simply cannot do it. I stopped washing the dishes and got down on my knees in front of Mace. I took his dirty little hands in mine and tried so desperately to reach him.

"Mason, I love you. I love you. If only you could understand how much I love you."

He just stared. He couldn't understand; he didn't comprehend. I stood up and started on the dishes again, but that didn't last long. This sense of urgency—almost a panic—came over me, and once more I dried my hands and knelt in front of my precious little boy.

"My dear Mason, if only you could say to me, 'I love you, Mother.' I need that, Mace."

Nothing.

I stood up to the sink again. More dishes, more washing, more crying—and thoughts, foreign to my way of thinking, began filtering into my conscious awareness. I believe God spoke to me that day, and this is what He said: *"Anabel, you don't look at your son and turn away in disgust because he's sitting there with saliva drooling out of his mouth; you don't shake your head, repulsed because he has dinner all over his shirt or because he's sitting in a dirty, smelly diaper when he ought to be able to take care of himself. Anabel, you don't reject Mason because all of the dreams you had for him have been destroyed. You don't reject him because he doesn't perform for you. You love him, Anabel, just because he is yours. Mason doesn't willfully reject your love, but you willfully reject Mine. I love you, Anabel, not because you're neat or attractive or because you do things well, not because you perform for Me but just because you're Mine."*[18]

Hearing Anabel's story transformed my thinking about God's love for me. For years I lived as though I had to be "good enough" for God to love me. I understood that salvation was a gift of grace—a free gift from God that I did not earn—but somewhere I began to believe the lie that I had to perform properly to keep the gift. I feared if I was not good enough, He would take it back. But that is a lie.

I am good enough...because Jesus lives in me and the Holy Spirit works through me. And friend, so are you.

I'm Not Enough

I'm not _____ enough. You can fill in that blank with smart, talented, gifted, spiritual, or any number of positive attributes (and many of those we will cover in the pages of this book). But the root source of each one of those lies is rooted in "I'm not *good* enough." It is one of the enemy's favorite weapons, and he uses it to keep God's children in bondage to feelings of inferiority, insecurity, and inadequacy. The bottom line is, the enemy wants you to believe that you are "not enough." Period. But you are enough. You are enough and have been equipped and empowered to do everything God has called you to do.

It seems the message, "I'm not good enough to earn my way to heaven on my own," has been transformed into, "I'm not good enough...period." God created man and woman and said, "It is good." We are so valuable to God that He gave His only Son to restore our brokenness.

To be honest, I could have been the poster child for this lie. If feeling inadequate was an Olympic event, I would have been on the Wheaties box. It was the undercurrent of my entire existence until I finally realized who I was in Christ. Bible teacher Beth Moore said, "In the dead of the night when insecurities crawl on us like fleas, all of us have terrifying bouts of insecurity and panics of insignificance.

Our human natures pitifully fall to the temptation to pull out the tape measure and gauge ourselves against people who seem more gifted and anointed by God."[19]

Many women are living in silent defeat, comparing themselves to other women who likewise are living in secret defeat. *I'm not a good mother. I'm not a good wife. I'm not a good Christian. I'm not a good witness. I'm not a good housekeeper. I'm not a good decorator. I'm not a good cook. I'm not a good...*

One by one the petals fall from the beautiful flower God created us to be. Like ticker tape, our fragmented pieces of confidence scatter over the streets as the parade passes by.

Unfortunately, I wasted many precious years held captive by the enemy's lies before I held up my chained hands to God and said, "I'm ready for you to set me free."

Consider this:

Jacob was a liar.

Moses was a stutterer.

Gideon was a coward.

David was an adulterer.

Rahab was a prostitute.

Esther was an orphan.

Balaam's donkey was...well, a donkey.

And yet God used each one of them to further His kingdom.

God doesn't call us because we are gifted or talented. He uses us because we are obedient and dependent on Him. He doesn't call the qualified; He qualifies the called.

The truth is, if you have experienced new birth in Christ, when God looks at you, He sees Jesus. And friend, Jesus is good enough.

Good Enough

OK. Perhaps you do believe that you are good enough for God. Perhaps you believe that when God looks at you, He sees Jesus. But now what? Do you believe that you are good enough to serve Him here on earth? Do you believe that because of Jesus in you, you are good enough to do whatever He has called you to do? Do you believe that you have powerful potential just waiting to be released? Oh dear sister, this is so important. (I'm praying the tears dripping on my keyboard don't cause an electrical short.) We have to understand that now that we are in Christ…*we are good enough to do whatever He calls us to do.* Far too many brothers and sisters in Christ are held back by the lie that they are not good enough to be all that God has called them to be. I know…I was one of them.

Just as I began to emerge from my cocoon of inferiority, insecurity, and inadequacy that was spun from many years of believing the lies, God began to give me a glimpse of the plans He had for me. Like a groundhog shrinking back in his hole for another six weeks of winter, I cried, "I'm not good enough. Get someone else." That's when God began to show me a whole passel of folks who felt the same way.

Moses was one of history's great leaders. After being raised in Pharaoh's household as his adopted grandson, he reached forty years of age and decided that he was ready to save the Israelite nation from slavery. His plan failed miserably. After Moses killed an Egyptian taskmaster, Pharaoh sought to take Moses' life in exchange. The once mighty man of words and deeds fled the palace and hid in the land of Midian.

For the next forty years, Moses took care of dirty, smelly sheep. He was so insecure that he developed a speech impediment and preferred the company of sheep to people. It was then, at Moses' lowest point in life, that God decided that he was ready for leadership. God appeared to Moses in a burning bush and called him to lead the Israelite nation out of Egypt.

"Moses! Moses!" God called when He saw that Moses had gone over to look at the burning bush.

"Here I am," Moses replied.

But "here I am" did not mean "here I am to do what you've called me to do." Moses argued fervently with God's plan to use him to lead the Israelite nation to freedom. "You've got the wrong person. I can't even speak without stuttering. Have you considered my brother, Aaron?" Four times Moses said, "What if this happens, what if this happens, what if this happens..." And each time God answered, "I will do it for you."

That is the same answer God gives us today. See, when Moses thought he was ready at age forty, he wasn't. When he thought he wasn't ready at age eighty, he was. When are we ready to do the impossible for God? We are ready when He calls us and when we know that we cannot do anything in our own strength but only by the power of God working in us. We *are* good enough when God's power is at work within us. Once Moses believed that God would do the leading, he had the confidence to start moving.

Gideon is another mighty warrior who argued with God's call. When God came to Gideon to appoint him the next leader of the Israelite army, he was busy in a winepress threshing wheat. Now, friend, you don't usually thresh wheat in a winepress. You thresh wheat by throwing it up in the air in an open field and letting the wind blow away the chaff. So what was he doing in the winepress? Gideon was so terrified of his enemies, he was hiding. And yet, when the angel of the Lord came to him, he addressed Gideon as "O valiant warrior!" (Judges 6:12 NASB). Can't you just see Gideon looking around and saying, "You talkin' to me?"

Yet, God called him "valiant warrior" because He knew what Gideon could be if he trusted in God's power to work through him.

Then there's one of the most powerful leaders of all time—King David. When the prophet Samuel went to Jesse's house to anoint the next king of Israel, he asked to see each of Jesse's sons. One by one the strapping young men paraded before Samuel for inspection, but God rejected them all even though Samuel thought Eliab looked like king material. But God told Samuel, "Do not consider [Eliab's] appearance or his height, for I have rejected him. The LORD does not look at the things man looks at. Man looks at the outward appearance, but the LORD looks at the heart" (1 Samuel 16:7).

Confused, Samuel asked Jesse, "Is that it? Don't you have any more sons?"

"Well, I do have one more son," Jesse said. "David is out in the field taking care of the sheep." David was the youngest of the bunch, and it never crossed Jesse's mind that he would be a candidate for king.

But when the young lad was brought in, God gave Samuel the thumbs up.

What about women in the Bible? If you were God and were going to list only five women in the lineage of Jesus, whom would you choose? I'd perhaps select Mrs. Noah, Mrs. Moses, or the lovely Mrs. Abraham. But God had a different idea. In Matthew chapter one, in addition to Mary, He listed Tamar, who had an incestuous encounter with her father-in-law; Rahab, who had been a prostitute; Ruth, who was a foreigner from a cursed land; and Bathsheba, who had an affair with King David. These are not the women we would likely choose, but it is a wonderful example of 1 Corinthians 1:26-31, which says that God deliberately seeks out the weak things and the despised things because it is from them that He can receive the greatest glory. To God, they were good enough.

God's Extraordinary Work through Ordinary People

God chooses to do extraordinary work through ordinary people who will bring glory to His name. It is through men and women who know they are not good enough in their own strength but incredibly powerful in God's strength who slay the giants of this world.

Once we take those first steps of obedience, it is crucial to remember that it is God who will bring the results. I love this account of one of the most famous preachers in the nineteenth century, Charles Spurgeon.

Charles Spurgeon was by all accounts the greatest preacher in the capital of the most powerful nation on earth. Huge throngs, including the wealthy and powerful, came to London's cavernous Metropolitan Tabernacle to hear him preach.

Spurgeon held himself to towering standards, always feeling his best wasn't good enough. One day, his worst fears were realized when he preached an awful sermon. He was so traumatized by his poor work that he rushed home and fell to his knees. "O Lord, I'm so feeble and You're so powerful!" he prayed. "Only You can make something of such a ghastly sermon. Please use it and bless it."

You or I might have told him to put his failure behind him and move on, but Spurgeon kept praying all week for God to use this terrible sermon. Meanwhile, he set about to do better the following Sunday. And he did. At the conclusion of that sermon, the audience of thousands all but carried him out on their shoulders.

But Spurgeon was not to be fooled. He decided to keep careful records of the results of the two sermons. Within a few months that outcome was clear. The "ghastly" sermon had led forty-one people to know Christ; his masterpiece had led to no observable results at all.[20]

When Spurgeon thought he was good enough in his own strength, he wasn't. When he thought he wasn't good enough, God was. God is able to do exceedingly abundantly more than we could ask or think (Ephesians 3:20). How amazing that He chooses to do it through us.

Unshakable Confidence

"I'm not good enough" is an insidious lie that the enemy whispers in our ears. It *is* a lie. It is not the truth.

The truth is, if you have made Jesus the Lord of your life, then you have the power of the Holy Spirit living in you and working through you. Jesus said, "You will receive power when the Holy Spirit comes on you" (Acts 1:8). You have God's incomparably great power at your disposal. "That power is like the working of his mighty strength, which he exerted in Christ when he raised him from the dead and seated him at his right hand in the heavenly realms" (Ephesians 1:19-20). The same power that raised Jesus from the dead is at work within us? Yep. The same power.

Jesus said, "I tell you the truth [Don't you just love it when He says that?], anyone who has faith in me will do what I have been doing. He will do even greater things than these because I am going to the Father" (John 14:12). What does going to the Father have to do with the power we receive? Because once Jesus went to the Father, the Holy Spirit came to live in believers. "If you love me, you will obey what I command. And I will ask the Father, and he will give you another Counselor to be with you forever—the Spirit of truth" (John 14:15-17).

Holocaust survivor Corrie ten Boom spent the last years of her life speaking to men and women all around the world about the God who sustained her during her imprisonment and who delivered her from the Nazi prison camps. During one of her presentations, she held up a lady's white glove.

> "What can this white glove do?" she asked. "The glove can do nothing. Oh, but if my hand is in the glove, it can do many things…cook, play the piano, write. Well, you say that is not the glove but the hand in the glove that does it. Yes, that is so. I tell you that we are nothing but gloves. The hand in the glove is the Holy Spirit of God. Can the glove do something if it is very near the hand? No. The glove must be filled with the hand to do the work. That is exactly the same for us: We must be filled with the Holy Spirit to do the work God has for us to do."[21]

I'm about to say something that is almost dangerous. It is hard for me to even believe myself. But when we say, "I'm not good enough," that is like saying that Jesus is not good enough or the Holy Spirit is not good enough. Jesus is in us (John 14:20). The Holy Spirit is in us (John 14:18). Are they good enough? Absolutely.

It's time to see yourself as God sees you. No more house of mirrors with a distorted image of who you are. This is how God sees you.

- You are a child of God—John 1:12
- You are justified completely—Romans 5:1
- You are free from condemnation—Romans 8:1
- You have the mind of Christ—1 Corinthians 2:16

- You have been made righteous—2 Corinthians 5:21
- You have been blessed with every spiritual blessing—Ephesians 1:3
- You are righteous and holy—Ephesians 4:24
- You have been redeemed and forgiven of all your sins—Colossians 1:14
- You are a dwelling place for Christ; He lives in you—Colossians 1:27
- You are complete in Christ—Colossians 2:10
- You are chosen of God, holy and dearly loved—Colossians 3:12
- You have been given a spirit of power, love, and self-discipline—2 Timothy 1:7
- You are a partaker of God's divine nature—2 Peter 1:4

And that, my friend, is only the beginning. Say these verses out loud. Speak to your soul. Believe the truth about who you are. You are more than good enough because of who lives in you and works through you.

Paul said that he "put no confidence in the flesh" (Philippians 3:3). In other words, he didn't think he was good enough because of any talent or ability he had. But his confidence came from who he was, what he had, and where he was as a child of God. Someone once said, "A man wrapped up in himself makes a pretty small package." But a man, or woman, wrapped up in God is an amazing sight to behold.

I am not advocating confidence in self, but confidence in God—confidence in who you are because of what Jesus has done for you and the Holy Spirit can do through you. Jesus said, "I am the vine; you are the branches. If you remain in me and I in you, you will bear much fruit; apart from me you can do nothing" (John 15:5-6 TNIV). Connected to the vine you can do everything God calls you to do (Philippians 4:13).

Paul knew what he could accomplish on his own—nothing. Oh, he could be busy. We all can do that. But bearing "fruit that will remain" is another story. This is how he viewed his personal weaknesses:

> Because of the extravagance of those revelations, and so I wouldn't get a big head, I was given the gift of a handicap to keep me in constant touch with my limitations. Satan's angel did his best to get me down; what he in fact did was push me to my knees. No danger then of walking around high and mighty! At first I didn't think of it as a gift, and begged God to remove it. Three times I did that, and then he told me,
>
> My grace is enough; it's all you need.
>
> My strength comes into its own in your weakness.
>
> Once I heard that, I was glad to let it happen. I quit focusing on the handicap and began appreciating the gift. It was a case of Christ's strength moving in on my weakness. Now I take limitations in stride, and with good cheer, these limitations that cut me down to size—abuse, accidents, opposition, bad breaks. I just let Christ take over! And so the weaker I get, the stronger I become (2 Corinthians 12:7-10 MSG).

A confident person is one who walks in faith. We walk in faith that we are holy, chosen, redeemed, dearly loved children of God who are empowered by the Holy Spirit, equipped by our Maker, and enveloped by Jesus Christ.

Lame Man Dancing

One summer my husband and I escaped to the captivating island of Bermuda where the water is crystal clear and the bluest of blues, and the air is filled with the scent of blooming hibiscus. The vacation was complete with long romantic walks on white sandy beaches, splashing waves on limestone rock jetties, and discoveries of secluded ocean-carved caves. At night, a million tiny green Bermuda tree frogs sang romantic cadences just for us.

One evening, Steve and I ate at a five-star restaurant filled with men and women dressed in their finest evening apparel. The semicircular dining room was lined with glass and overlooked the Atlantic Ocean, allowing the flaming orange red of the setting sun to be our backdrop.

In one corner of the dining area, a four-man orchestra filled the room with music from the forties and fifties. Steve and I had taken a few ballroom dance lessons, and he said, "Come on, Sharon. Let's take a spin on the dance floor and see if we can remember the fox-trot."

"No way," I said. "Nobody else is out there. I'm not going to be the only one on the floor with everyone staring at me. Let's wait until there are some other people dancing. Then I'll go."

Finally another couple approached the floor. They looked like professional dancers, moving as one and never missing a beat. This did not encourage me at all, but only strengthened my resolve that this was no place for my feet to tread.

Then couple number one was joined by couple number two, whose steps weren't quite as perfect.

"OK, now I'll go," I said. "But let's get in the back corner where nobody can see us."

So off we went to our little spot on the dance floor and tried to remember the 1-2-3-4s of the fox-trot. As we were moving as two, I noticed a fourth couple approach the floor. They came with confidence—no hesitation, no timidity. But there was something special about this couple. The man was in a wheelchair.

He was a middle-aged, slightly balding man with a neatly trimmed beard. On his left hand he wore a white glove, I guessed to cover a skin disease. Both were dressed in their evening wear, but the most beautiful part of their dress was their radiant smiles. Their love for each other lit up the room.

As the band played a peppy beat, the wife held her love's healthy right hand and danced with him. He never did rise from the wheelchair, but they didn't seem to care. They came together and separated like expert dancers. He spun her around as she stooped to conform to his seated position. Lovingly, like a little fairy child, she danced around his chair while his laughter became the fifth instrument in this small orchestra. Even though his feet did not move from their metal resting place, his shoulders swayed in perfect time and his eyes danced with hers.

My heart was so moved that I had to bury my face on Steve's shoulder so no one would see the tears streaming down my cheeks. I noticed that all around the room linen napkins were dabbing tearful eyes. Even the band was transfixed by this portrait of love and devotion.

Then the music slowed to a lazy romantic melody. The wife pulled a chair up beside her husband, and they held each other in a dancers' embrace. Cheek to cheek they swayed to the piano man's romantic love song. At one point they both closed their eyes and, I imagined, dreamed of an earlier time when they were not restrained by his chair.

After watching this incredible display of love and courage, I realized that my inhibitions of not wanting others to watch me because my steps were not perfect were gone. The Lord spoke to my heart in a powerful way.

"Sharon, who moved this crowd to tears? Was it couple number one with their perfect steps? Or was it the last couple who not only did not have perfect steps, but had no steps at all? No, My child, it was the display of love, not perfection, that had an effect on the people watching. If you obey Me, I will do it for you just as his wife did it for him."

For several months I had been praying about whether to answer God's call to become vice president and radio cohost of an international women's ministry. I had argued with God, telling Him that I was not qualified—that I was not "good enough" to serve. I assured Him He had made a mistake in choosing me. But just as He answered Moses' arguments, God answered mine. He said, "I will do it for you."

My steps will never be perfect, on a dance floor or, more importantly, in life. But the Lord doesn't expect my steps to be perfect. He just expects me to listen to His voice, to be obedient, to take the first step of faith, and to let Him do the rest. The man in the wheelchair never moved his feet, but his wife did the moves for him. And I need to remember that the Lord will do it for me.

I also need to remember that it is not perfect steps that the world is so desperately looking for. They aren't impressed by perfect people who live in perfect houses with perfect children. They are impressed by love. Genuine, God-inspired love. That's what moves a crowd.

That night, by the beautiful shores of Bermuda, the Lord sent a lame man to teach me how to dance. I don't have to worry about being good enough. I simply need to walk in tandem with God, or in this case dance to His lead, and He will do it for me.

And He will do it for you.

● ● ● **RECOGNIZE THE LIE:** I'm not good enough.

● ● ● **REJECT THE LIE:** That's not true.

● ● ● **REPLACE THE LIE WITH TRUTH:**

- "On that day, you will realize that I [Jesus] am in the Father, and you are in me, and I am in you" (John 14:20).

- "But you were washed, you were sanctified, you were justified in the name of the Lord Jesus Christ and by the Spirit of our God" (1 Corinthians 6:11).

- "For we are God's workmanship, created in Christ Jesus to do good works, which God prepared in advance for us to do" (Ephesians 2:10).

- "His divine power has given us everything we need for life and godliness through our knowledge of him who called us by his own glory and goodness. Through these he has given us his very great and precious promises, so that through them you may participate in the divine nature and escape the corruption in the world caused by evil desires" (2 Peter 1:3-4).

7

I'm Worthless

LIE: *I'm worthless.*

TRUTH: *I am God's treasured possession (Deuteronomy 14:2).*

April felt unacceptable, unlovable, and unworthy of God's love. She longed to know what God really thought of her—what He saw when He looked at her.

"Lord, please speak to me and tell me how You see me?" she prayed. "I feel so worthless."

A few days after April cried out to God, He reminded her of a special field day in elementary school. It was as if God had pushed the "play" button on the movie screen of her memory. April was ten years old, lined up for the 100-yard-dash on her Christian school playground. All the other kids had on their school-issued navy uniforms, but she wore a pair of bright orange, green, and yellow striped culottes with matching top.

The whistle blew, and April took off running as fast as she could. She left the other girls in the dust and crossed the finish line first.

From several yards away, April's big brother and his friends watched the event from the second-story window of the high school. "Did you see your little sister win that race?" one of the boys asked.

"Are you kidding?" he said. "I couldn't miss her with those stripes."

"Later, when he told my parents the story," April recalled, "he seemed so proud of me. He said, 'You should have seen her. There was a long line of blue and then a flash of color running way ahead of them. She was amazing!'"

April asked God what He was trying to tell her by bringing this childhood memory into view.

"That is how I see you," He seemed to say. "You stand out above all the rest. You don't have to fit in with all the others and be what they say you should be. I am proud of you, just like your brother was proud of you that day. Don't be afraid of being different. I made you unique in every way. I love you just the way you are. You are a blue-ribbon winner. You are My treasured possession."

Valued and Adored

Another common lie that women believe today is that they are worthless. They believe demeaning words they have heard from childhood: from careless parents, unthinking friends, tactless teachers, and imprudent peers.

But this is not a new problem. In biblical times, Pharisees prayed each day, "God, I thank You that I am not a Gentile or a woman."

But how does God feel about that?

God elevates women. As we saw earlier in Genesis, God created both man and woman in His image. And in the New Testament, we see a number of women interacting with Jesus and carrying out valuable roles in His ministry.

The longest recorded conversation with Jesus was with—you guessed it—a woman. Jesus went out of his way to talk to this Samaritan woman as she drew water from a well. This was a woman who had been married and divorced five times, and the man she was currently living with was not her husband. She felt worthless, but Jesus came to tell her otherwise. He went out of His way to set her free.

A man speaking to a woman in public, especially a Samaritan, was socially unacceptable in those days. But Jesus engaged her in conversation and even asked her for a drink. None of that was lost on her: "You are a Jew and I am a Samaritan woman. How can you ask me for a drink?" (John 4:9). I imagine she used quite a sarcastic tone in response to his request. But Jesus continued to address her with love and compassion. He didn't merely want a drink for Himself; He wanted to give her everlasting water to quench her parched soul.

Jesus put Himself on her level. He looked her in the eye, spoke directly to her heart, and offered her the most incredible gift imaginable. It was the first time Jesus actually revealed His true identity to someone (4:26). She embraced God's amazing grace and then ran into town to share it with all she knew.

Let me give you another example. Oh, how I love this one. It occurred in the small Judean village of Bethany where Jesus' good friends Lazarus, Mary, and Martha lived. Jesus and His disciples stopped by for a visit and were invited to dinner. The house was a buzz of activity and hospitality flowed. But somewhere among the clatter of pots and pans, the pounding of barley and rye, the grinding of wheat and herbs, Mary wandered into the room filled with men. She plopped right down in the middle of the "men's club," got out her pen and paper (or would have if she had had them), and began to take in Jesus' every word. Mary became a disciple, a student of the Master.

To you and me, that doesn't seem like such a big deal. But back then it was momentous. Unheard of. Women were relegated to the kitchen, the bedroom, and the nursery. They did not socialize with the men, and they certainly did not sit in a room to be taught. This was not lost on Martha. She was furious.

> "Lord, doesn't it seem unfair to you that my sister just sits here while I do all the work? Tell her to come and help me."
>
> But the Lord said to her, "My dear Martha, you are worried and upset over all these details! There is only one thing worth being concerned about. Mary has discovered it, and *it will not be taken away from her*" (Luke 10:38-42 NLT, emphasis added).

Jesus was not going to tell Mary to leave the room. He welcomed her as a disciple, as one being taught.

Again, when Jesus was resurrected from the dead, the first person He appeared to in the garden was a woman, Mary Magdalene (John 20:1-18).

A premorning mist hovered over the garden surrounding the tomb where Jesus' body had been laid three days earlier. Mary Magdalene stood by the tomb, mourning the death of her beloved Jesus. But then, as she blinked to readjust her eyes, she noticed the unthinkable. The massive stone had been rolled away from the entrance to Jesus' grave.

How could this be? Mary thought to herself. *Who would have stolen His body?*

Mary ran back to tell the disciples what she had seen. Peter and John raced to the empty tomb and discovered the abandoned burial cloths that had once been wrapped around the Savior's body. Bewildered, the men went back to report what they had seen. But Mary stayed behind, weeping for the One she loved.

When she looked in the tomb, she saw two angels who asked her, "Woman, why are you crying?"

"They have taken my Lord away," Mary replied through her tears, "and I don't know where they have put Him."

Hearing a rustling in the myrtle bushes behind her, Mary turned her head. There appeared another figure, as if in a dream.

"Woman, why are you weeping?" the man asked.

Mary thought the man was the gardener. "Sir, if you know where they have taken Jesus, would you please tell me so that I can take care of Him?"

Then Jesus said one simple word: "Mary."

At the sound of her name, Mary recognized Jesus.

I don't know why Jesus didn't reveal himself to Peter and John when they arrived at the tomb. I don't know why He didn't go to the discouraged disciples straight away. But I am deeply moved that He appeared to this woman in the garden before He made his grand debut to the world. He honored her with His appearance. He trusted her with His message. He valued her as a precious friend.

Dear one, Jesus is calling your name. He makes Himself known to you. He reveals Himself to you. He is calling your name. You are valued and adored.

Touched and Healed

There was another woman who believed she was absolutely worthless (Mark 5:25-34). For twelve years she had suffered from bleeding, and no one could find a cure. The more money she spent on treatment, the worse her condition grew. Her money was gone; her heart was spent. During Jesus' day, a woman was considered "unclean" during her monthly period. This woman had been "unclean" for twelve years. Untouchable. Unacceptable. Worthless.

But she had heard about this Jesus. "He heals the sick. He raises the dead. He restores sight to the blind." *Perhaps He could heal me,* she hoped.

Can you see her? Her head was covered. Her eyes downcast. Hoping no one would recognize her as she scurried through the crowd.

If I could just touch the hem of His garment. I know I'm not supposed to be out in public, but I have nowhere else to turn. There He is! I see Him!

Thinking that she could "steal" a healing, the woman reached through the crowd and touched the corner of Jesus' robe. Immediately, her bleeding stopped.

But what happened next was even more miraculous than the physical healing she received. Jesus halted the caravan of followers to recognize one who felt worthless in the world's eyes.

As soon as the healing power left Jesus' body, He spun around and asked, "Who touched my clothes?"

The disciples thought that was a strange question. Hundreds of people were pressing in all around him. How could he ask, "Who touched my clothes?" But Jesus always knows the intentions of our hearts, and He distinguished the touch of faith from the touch of followers.

The woman could have easily snuck away with her healing. But

Jesus was interested in her total restoration not simply her physical health. With fear and trembling, she fell at her Healer's feet.

"It was I," she cried. "I know I am not worthy to wipe the dust from your feet, but I have had an issue of blood for these twelve years. You were my only hope. Forgive me, Lord."

"Daughter, your faith has healed you. Go in peace and be freed from your suffering" (Mark 5:34).

Yes, He was on His way to an important official's home. Jairus' daughter was dying, and Jesus was about to make an important house call. And yet, this daughter of Abraham was also important to Him. He stopped His journey, turned about face, and restored her physically, emotionally, and spiritually. She was worth it. And so are you.

Battered and Bruised

The speaker came on stage and pulled out a $100 bill.

"Who would like this $100 bill?" he asked.

Hands shot up all around the room.

Then he crumpled the bill, threw it on the floor, and ground it with his foot. Holding up the dirty and tattered money, he then asked, "Now, who wants this $100 bill?"

The same hands went into the air.

"And that is why God still wants you," he said. "You may be battered and bruised. You may be tattered and torn. You may be crumpled and creased. But that doesn't change your value to God any more than what I've done changes the value of this money. You are still precious and valuable to the God who chose you, redeemed you, and loves you as His own."

> As a father has compassion on his children,
>   so the LORD has compassion on those who fear him;
>   for he knows how we are formed,
>   he remembers that we are dust
>   (Psalm 103:13-14).

God understands that we are fatally flawed creatures, yet He deems us immeasurably valuable no matter how crumbled and soiled we are.

Jars of Clay

Paul wrote to the Christians at Corinth, "But we have this treasure in jars of clay to show that this all-surpassing power is from God and not from us" (2 Corinthians 4:7). You and I might not look like much on the outside—we may appear as common clay jars—but inside are hidden incredible treasures. Inside these old cracked pots reside the most incredible treasure of all: Jesus Christ. And that makes us valuable.

In Louisa May Alcott's book, *Little Women,* Mrs. March says to her three girls, Meg, Jo, and Amy, "I only care what you think of yourself. If you feel your value lies in being merely decorative, I fear that someday you might find yourself believing that's all you really are. Time erodes all such beauty. But what it cannot diminish is the wonderful workings of your mind—your humor, your kindness, and your moral courage. These are things I so cherish in you."

Our culture places an ungodly amount of significance on a woman's appearance. Outward trappings are simply that—trappings. But God sees us as simple jars of clay containing valuable treasure…and that makes us beautiful to Him.

Priceless Pigs

An African tribe viewed *The Jesus Film* in their own language. As a follow-up, another ministry, Faith Comes by Hearing, provided the tribe with an Audio Bible and a digital playback unit.[22] A group gathered round to listen to the story of Jesus healing a demon-possessed man recorded in Luke 8.

> [Jesus and his disciples] sailed to the region of the Gerasenes, which is across the lake from Galilee. When Jesus stepped ashore, he was met by a demon-possessed man from the town. For a long time this man had not worn clothes or lived in a house, but had lived in the tombs. When he saw Jesus, he cried out and fell at

his feet, shouting at the top of his voice, "What do you want with me, Jesus, Son of the Most High God? I beg you, don't torture me!" For Jesus had commanded the evil spirit to come out of the man. Many times it had seized him, and though he was chained hand and foot and kept under guard, he had broken his chains and had been driven by the demon into solitary places.

Jesus commanded the demons to come out of the man and cast them into a herd of nearby pigs. The pigs then rushed down a steep hillside and into a lake and were drowned.

The tribal community was stunned when they heard this story. They knew the value of one pig, much less an entire herd. Why would Jesus do that? Why would He allow their entire income to be destroyed?

Many questions stirred among the listeners. Then the wise chief spoke. "Perhaps Jesus is showing us that one human soul is worth more than an entire tribe's economy."

I was silenced by his answer. That passage has been mysterious to me for many years, but God revealed the truth to an African chief hearing the story for the very first time. That chief understood just how valuable we are to God.

Life Without Limbs

The camera framed the young man's handsome face as he flashed a smile to the audience and said, "My name is Nick Vujicic, and I'm from Australia. This morning, I want to share my testimony as to how God has given me grace, strength, and comfort through my disability and how you can have victory, peace, and joy in your life even if your circumstances don't make sense or cause your world to turn upside down."

The camera pulled back to reveal a young man with no arms and no legs, sitting before a mesmerized audience. Several video clips followed as we watched him shaving, getting a glass of water, walking up stairs, and diving headfirst into a swimming pool.

Born with no limbs, Nick has one of the most powerful of all human attributes: a voice. He has made over 1,600 speaking appearances in 12 nations. "No matter who you are, no matter what you're going through, God knows it," he said. "He is with you. He is going to pull you through."

I watched as Nick spoke to Dr. Robert Schuller during a worship service at the Crystal Cathedral in California. Nick is a twenty-four-year old dynamo. He told the story of his early years living a life without limbs. There was no medical reason why he was born as he was, but Nick believes that he is fearfully and wonderfully made. He knows that God has a unique plan for his life.

On his left side, Nick has a tiny foot with two toes at the end of a stub. He calls it a "chicken drumstick" because that's what it looks like. With that tiny foot and two toes, Nick can type 43-words per minute on a keyboard. He has a double degree in accounting and financial planning, can walk, swim, and bring a crowd to its knees with his amazing words of God's grace.

"My purpose in life is to go out in the world and say, 'If I can trust in God with my circumstances, then you can trust in God with your circumstances.' We know that God's grace is sufficient, and if He doesn't answer your prayers, just know that He is with you and that's the message—'Fear not, for I am with you.' "

Nick reminded viewers that we should not compare sufferings. It's not about what we can do or cannot do. It's about what we become by the power of Jesus Christ no matter our circumstances.

Nick wasn't always so positive. When he was eight years old, he wanted to kill himself by flipping himself off the kitchen table to break his neck. His father was a pastor, and Nick grew up going to church and Sunday school. He learned the verses in Psalm 139 that said he was fearfully and wonderfully made. He read Jeremiah 29:11 about how God had a future and a hope for his life. *What kind of future will I have?* he wondered.

He thought he would never get married, hold his wife's hand, dance on his wedding day, or be able to put his arms around his children when they cried. "These things were important to me," he said.

"No one could tell me that everything was going to be OK. And even if they did, I couldn't believe them."

Not yet in his teens, Nick prayed that God would give him arms and legs. "It said in the Bible, 'Ask and you shall receive.' I had faith, and I was actually very angry at God. I didn't understand it. And I thought maybe I wasn't good enough. Maybe that's the reason He's not answering my prayer. I mean, arms and legs are nothing for God, the Creator of the universe. And so I prayed for my circumstance to change, but it didn't happen."

God did not give Nick arms and legs, but He gave him an incredible message of hope and purpose. Nick shows the world that the greatest joy we will ever experience is the joy of knowing Christ. In some countries, Nick would have been killed at birth. He would have been tossed away because of his physical defects. But Nick is not worthless. He is a global change agent and one of God's mighty men on assignment to tell a hurting world about the hope and healing of Jesus Christ. He is extremely valuable, incredibly precious, and exorbitantly priceless.

Here's what I want you to hear as I stand on my chair with a megaphone—hear this! "If the world thinks you're not good enough, it's a lie, you know," Nick says. "Get a second opinion."

Get a second opinion. Get God's opinion. He thinks Nick is amazing. He thinks you are amazing. Nick, with no arms and legs, thought he wasn't good enough for God to answer his prayers for physical wholeness. He felt worthless. But oh, God had a greater plan. He is using Nick to bring spiritual wholeness to millions around the world. That is amazing. Nick *is* good enough. Nick is enough. Nick is incredibly valuable to God.[23]

The Touch of the Master's Hand

Myra was a woman battered and scarred from severe arthritis. Her legs were held captive in a wheelchair, but her soul was forever free. With one pencil in each crippled hand, she used the erasers to type words on her typewriter. The joy of her efforts in typing the words outweighed the pain of creating them.

One day, when a friend was leaving Myra's home, she patted her wheelchair and said, "And I thank God for this!" Prior to her wheelchair days, Myra's talent had been hidden like a treasure in the sand. But after the crippling effect of arthritis confined her, the talent locked away freed her. And God used one of her most precious poems to show me our incredible worth.

"The Touch of the Master's Hand"

It was battered and scarred,
And the auctioneer thought it
Hardly worth his while
To waste his time on the old violin,
But he held it up with a smile.

"What am I bid, good people," he cried,
"Who starts the bidding for me?
One dollar, one dollar, do I hear two?
Two dollars, who makes it three?
Three dollars once, three dollars twice, going for three."

But, No,
From the room far back a grey-haired man
Came forward and picked up the bow.
Then wiping the dust from the old violin
And tightening up the strings,
He played a melody, pure and sweet,
As sweet as the angel sings.

The music ceased and the auctioneer
With a voice that was quiet low,
Said, "What now am I bid for this old violin?"
As he held it aloft with its bow.
"One thousand, one thousand, do I hear two?

Two thousand, who makes it three?
Three thousand once, three thousand twice,
Going and gone," said he.

The audience cheered,
But some of them cried,
"We just don't understand.
What changed its worth?"
Swift came the reply,
"The Touch of the Master's Hand."

And many a man with life out of tune,
All battered with bourbon and gin,
Is auctioned cheap to a thoughtless crowd
Much like that old violin.
A mess of pottage, a glass of wine,
A game and he travels on.
He is going once, he is going twice,
He is going and almost gone.
But the Master comes,
And the foolish crowd never can quite understand,
The worth of a soul and the change that is wrought
By the Touch of the Master's Hand.

—Myra Brooks Welch

••• **Recognize the lie:** I'm worthless.

••• **Reject the lie:** That is not true.

••• **Replace the lie with truth:**

- "'Look at the birds of the air; they do not sow or reap or store away in barns, and yet your heavenly Father feeds them. Are you not much more valuable than they?'" (Matthew 6:26).
- "Don't you know that you yourselves are God's temple and that God's Spirit lives in you?" (1 Corinthians 3:16).

- "Praise be to the God and Father of our Lord Jesus Christ, who has blessed us in the heavenly realms with every spiritual blessing in Christ. For he chose us in him before the creation of the world to be holy and blameless in his sight. In love he predestined us to be adopted as his sons through Jesus Christ, in accordance with his pleasure and will" (Ephesians 1:3-5).

8

I'm a Failure

Lie: *I'm a failure.*

Truth: *I can do all things through Christ who gives me strength (Philippians 4:13).*

June was a senior on the debate team when she presented a pro-life argument. She did her research and displayed amazing pictures of the development of a child in his mother's womb. She won the debate and received the highest grade possible. Six months later she had her first abortion.

Simply knowing the truth does not assure that we will walk in the truth. June knew the truth in her head, but did not have the courage to apply it to her life. "I could not speak what I supposedly believed any longer," June lamented. "I was a defeated failure." June went on to have two more abortions while attending college and eventually dropped out of school. Pregnant for the fourth time, she packed her bags and went home to her parents. As far as they knew, this was her first pregnancy.

This time, June knew she would have her baby…and she did.

Peter, the apostle, and June walked a similar path. While June denied her children the right to live, Peter denied his Savior's Lordship.

During the last meal Jesus celebrated with His disciples before He faced the cross, Jesus warned them that He would be leaving soon.

"Lord, where are you going?" Peter asked.

Jesus replied, "Where I am going, you cannot follow now, but you will follow later."

Peter asked, "Lord, why can't I follow you now? I will lay down my life for you. Even if all fall away on account of you, I never will" (John 13:37, Matthew 26:33).

Then Jesus answered, "Will you really lay down your life for me? I tell you the truth, before the rooster crows, you will disown me three times!" (John 13:38).

But Peter declared, "Even if I have to die with you, I will never disown you" (Matthew 26:35).

I imagine Jesus simply looked at Peter with a knowing eye and a wounded heart. *Sure you will, buddy,* He must have mused. *You will die with Me, but not today.*

Peter was so sure of himself, and yet, before the sun rose over the horizon, he did the very opposite of what his self-assured, overconfident words proclaimed.

"You are not one of His disciples, are you?" a girl asked at the door to the high priest's courtyard.

"I am not," Peter said.

"You are not one of his disciples, are you?" someone asked as Peter stood warming his hands by the fire.

"I am not," Peter said.

"Didn't I see you with Jesus in the olive grove, and aren't you the fellow who cut off my relative's ear?" challenged another.

"I am not!" Peter said for a third time.

The moment the third denial escaped Peter's lips, a rooster crowed. As the new day broke over the horizon, Peter's heart broke over his sin. Peter wept bitterly over his cowardly actions. This brash, boisterous, demonstrative fisherman had cowered under the accusing gaze of a mere servant girl.

I am fearful that we have put this story on a shelf for safekeeping. We believers tend to follow the baseball rule book rather than God's Word when it comes to the failure of our brothers and sisters—three strikes and you're out. But the Umpire of the Universe calls it differently. He puts on the cloak of mercy and grace and invites us to get back in the game.

Back in the Game

Three days after Jesus had breathed his last earthly breath, the disciples received the news of the empty tomb from the women who had gone to visit the grave. Mark tells us an angel told the women to go and "tell the disciples and Peter" that Jesus was alive (Mark 16:7). I wonder why the angel singled out Peter? Could it be that God knew Peter would need an extra measure of grace and assurance because of his failure?

Can you imagine how Peter's heart raced as his feet ran to the empty tomb? I wonder what he was thinking as he kicked up the dust? Would he be ashamed to face Jesus if He were alive? Would he be grateful for another chance? Would Jesus even want to see him?

Peter did encounter Jesus after his resurrection. We don't know how many times they were together or the conversations that took place. But God does allow us to witness how Jesus embraced and restored this broken "rock."

After Jesus had appeared to the disciples and to many others, it seemed like life just went back to normal. Peter and John went back to doing what they had been used to...fishing. As the sun rose over the horizon one morning, their nets remained empty. A man called from the shore, "Friend, have you caught any fish?"

"No," they answered.

"Throw your net on the other side of the boat and you will find some."

As the nets began to fill, John remembered a similar incident three years earlier and realized it was Jesus on the shore.

Peter jumped in the water and swam to shore while the others hauled in the miraculous catch. After dinner, Jesus pulled Peter aside and asked him,

"Simon son of John, do you truly love me more than these?"

"Yes, Lord," he said, "you know that I love you."

Jesus said, "Feed my lambs."

Again Jesus said, "Simon son of John, do you truly love me?"

He answered, "Yes, Lord, you know that I love you."

Jesus said, "Take care of my sheep."

The third time he said to him, "Simon son of John, do you love me?"

Peter was hurt because Jesus asked him the third time, "Do you love me?" He said, "Lord, you know all things; you know that I love you."

Jesus said, "Feed my sheep" (John 21:15-17).

June felt much like Peter. "I denied Jesus each time I walked through the door of that abortion clinic," she said. "But He has pulled me aside and asked, 'June, do you love Me?' And I have answered as Peter, 'Yes, Lord, You know that I love You.'

"I had felt that I was too far gone for God to forgive me, but He showed me that there is no place that is too far away from His grace that He cannot save. My sin is not greater than God's grace."

Failure Misbelief

It is easy to think that one failure marks our identity as a failure. That is what the enemy wants us to believe. If he can make us feel as though we *are* a failure, then he's the winner.

Brennan Manning, in his book, *Abba's Child,* wrote: "It used to be that I never felt safe with myself unless I was performing flawlessly. My desire to be perfect had transcended my desire for God...My jaded perception of personal failure and inadequacy led to a loss of self-esteem, triggering episodes of mild depression and heavy anxiety."[24]

Failure is just part of life, and the sooner we accept that we are flawed humans who depend on the perfect Christ, the sooner we put the taskmaster of perfection away. I am not a failure, but I am a child of God who sometimes fails.

What is failure anyway, except a manmade yardstick for performance? God is much more interested in the process than the product. If I obey God and lose the sale, I am still a success in God's eyes.

Famous Failures

Perhaps it is not failure of a spiritual nature that has you bound. Perhaps it's failure of a marriage, of a job, of simple tasks that have influenced the perception that you are a failure. If so, consider this:

- After Fred Astaire's first screen test in 1933, the director noted, "Can't act. Slightly bald. Can dance a little."
- Louisa May Alcott, author of *Little Women,* was encouraged to find work as a servant or a seamstress.
- Beethoven's violin teacher once told him he was a "hopeless composer."
- Walt Disney was fired by a newspaper editor for lack of ideas.
- Thomas Edison's teacher said he was too stupid to learn anything.
- Albert Einstein didn't speak until he was four years old and didn't read until he was seven. His teachers describe him as mentally slow.
- Isaac Newton did poorly in grade school.
- Henry Ford failed and went bankrupt five times before he finally succeeded.
- Babe Ruth set the home-run record (714), but he also once held the record for the most strikeouts (1,330).
- Winston Churchill failed sixth grade.
- Dr. Seuss' first children's book, *And to Think that I Saw It on Mulberry Street,* was rejected by 27 publishers. The 28th publisher, Vanguard Press, sold six million copies of the book.
- In 1902, the poetry editor of the *Atlantic Monthly* returned the poems of a 28-year-old poet with the following note: "Our magazine has no room for your vigorous verse." The poet was Robert Frost.

- In 1889, Rudyard Kipling received the following rejection letter from the *San Francisco Examiner:* "I'm sorry, Mr. Kipling, but you just don't know how to use the English language."
- One basketball player missed 9,000 shots in his career. He lost more than 300 games. Twenty-six times he was trusted to take the game's winning shot and missed. His name is Michael Jordan. He said, "I've failed over and over again in my life. And that's why I succeed."

These people refused to believe they were a failure simply because they had failed. We need to reject the lie of the enemy that tries to kick us when we are down by telling us the lie. Failure can be the springboard for future success.

I'm thinking of one man who failed in business in '31, was defeated for the legislature and lost his job in '32, was elected to the legislature in '34 but had a nervous breakdown in '36, was defeated for speaker in '38, was defeated for elector in '40, was defeated for Congress in '43, was elected to Congress in '46 but defeated in '48, was defeated by less than 100 votes for the Senate in '50, was defeated for vice president in '56 and for the Senate in '58. But in 1860 Abraham Lincoln was elected president of the United Sates. After losing a Senate race, Lincoln said, "The path was worn and slippery. My foot slipped from under me, knocking the other out of the way, but I recovered and said to myself, 'It's a slip and not a fall.' "[25]

Once a little boy was practicing baseball by himself in the backyard. He threw the ball in the air, swung, and missed. Time and time again he missed the ball as it descended to the ground. Finally he huffed and said, "Man, that's some pitcher."

What a great perspective!

I Can't-itis

By the time my son was four years old he had a bad case of "I can't-itis." If he didn't have immediate success in an endeavor, his tendency was to throw up his chubby little hands and say, "I can't do it!"

When it came time to take the training wheels off his bike, a bad case of "I can't-itis" crept in. For several hours, Steven tried to balance on two wheels, but crashed to the ground time and time again. "I can't do it," he stormed.

"You can't do it *yet,*" I said. "But you will. And when you learn to ride your bike, it will be the *funnest* thing you do as a kid."

Steven looked me in the eye, placed his balled-up hands on his little hips, and slowly said, "This-is-not-fun-and-it-will-never-be-fun."

Oh, my, how I saw myself in those eyes. So many times when God is trying to teach me a life lesson or a new discipline, I lose my balance and want to quit. He takes the training wheels off and sets me on the road of maturity, and sometimes I tumble to the ground. "I can't do it," I cry. "This is not fun and it will never be fun."

But God just keeps on working with me, holding the back of the bicycle until I learn to balance and keep moving ahead. The next thing you know, I'm cruising down victory lane, and God is laughing with joy and delight.

A few days after Steven's declaration of defeat, he walked out the door, hopped on his little red bike, and peddled around the yard without losing his balance once. And you know what, riding his bicycle *was* the funnest thing he ever did as a kid.

A Boy Who Said "God Can"

When God spoke to Moses through the burning bush and called him to lead the Israelites out of Egyptian bondage, Moses was struck with a bad case of "I can't-itis."

"Please pick someone else," he cried.

But when God called a kid named David to slay a giant, he said, "God can do it through me." We meet this young shepherd boy during Saul's reign. The Israelites were at war with a powerful warrior people known as the Philistines. The two warring factions camped on opposing hillsides with a valley in between. It seemed the Philistines had a secret weapon named Goliath, who was over nine feet tall, wore a bronze helmet, and a bronze coat of mail that weighed 125 pounds.

For forty days, morning and evening, this nine-foot giant of a man approached the battle lines and shouted at the Israelites, taunting and challenging them to a two-man duel. God's chosen people were terrified and huddled together in fear.

One day, David's father instructed him to take some lunch over to three of his brothers who were huddling among the Israelite army. I can almost see him skipping along without a care in the world. He heard the war cries, left the provisions at the camp, and ran out to the battle lines to see what all the commotion was about. Just as he approached, Goliath came forward and shouted his usual defiant challenge. While the soldiers turned tail and ran, David stood there in a cloud of dust and asked: "Who is this uncircumcised Philistine that he should defy the armies of the living God?" (1 Samuel 17:26).

This young shepherd boy confidently declared, "Let no one lose heart on account of this Philistine; your servant will go and fight him...The LORD who delivered me from the paw of the lion and the paw of the bear will deliver me from the hand of this Philistine" (1 Samuel 17:32,37).

Oh, I love it. I love it! David refused Saul's heavy cumbersome armor, but gathered five smooth stones from a nearby stream. He stood as tall and erect as his lanky teenage legs could stand and shouted at the towering enemy,

> "You come against me with sword and spear and javelin, but I come against you in the name of the LORD Almighty, the God of the armies of Israel, whom you have defied. This day the LORD will hand you over to me, and I'll strike you down and cut off your head. Today I will give the carcasses of the Philistine army to the birds of the air and the beasts of the earth, and the whole world will know that there is a God in Israel. All those gathered here will know that it is not by sword or spear that the LORD saves; for the battle is the LORD's, and he will give all of you into our hands" (1 Samuel 17:45-47).

As Goliath began to move closer, David charged his enemy, placed a smooth stone in his sling, and took perfect aim. The stone sank into Goliath's forehead, and he fell facedown on the ground. Can't you just see the stunned Israelites, the shocked Philistines, and the smiling angels as David stood over the giant with his foot pressed against the armor-clad chest?

I'm about to start shouting right now. Go ahead. Give a shout for the home team!

Now this is what I want us to see. Moses was a man who cowered when God called him into leadership. David was a young man who took the bull by the horns, or rather the giant by the head, when faced with God's enemy. What made the difference? Moses looked at his abilities and said, "I can't. I don't have what it takes." David looked at the almighty God and said, "God can. He has what it takes."

No matter what you're facing today—no matter what giants are standing in your path—if God gives you the vision, He will give you the provision. He doesn't necessarily call the equipped, but He always equips the called. You have what it takes. God has given you the power of the Holy Spirit. That same power is what transformed Peter from a coward who denied he even knew Jesus into a courageous leader who spoke out with confidence and passion after Jesus' ascension.

Satan wants us to believe that we don't have what it takes. God's truth is that we have everything we need. The power of the Holy Spirit has been given to us, is living in us, and working through us. But here's the key. That power is *for us who believe* (Ephesians 1:18-20). The power is available, but we must believe to receive.

Satan tells me, "You can't."

God tells me, "I already have."

The only obstacle keeping us from doing all that God has called us to do and being all that God has called us to be is our unbelief. It was the same with the Israelites headed to the Promised Land and it's the same for you and me headed to ours. Jesus said, "All things are possible to those who believe."

If God has called you to it, He will see you through it. The truth is: "I can do everything through Christ who gives me strength."

A Funeral for "I Can't"

Chick Moorman was observing various classrooms when he stumbled into Donna's fourth-grade class. It looked like a traditional elementary classroom, yet something seemed different the day he entered it for the first time. There seemed to be an undercurrent of excitement. Let's hear from Chick as he tells what he saw that day.

Donna was a veteran small-town Michigan school-teacher only two years away from retirement. In addition she was a volunteer participant in a country-wide staff development project I had organized and facilitated. The training focused on language arts ideas that would empower students to feel good about themselves and take charge of their lives. Donna's job was to attend training sessions and implement the concepts being presented. My job was to make classroom visitations and encourage implementation.

I took an empty seat in the back of the room and watched. All the students were working on a task, filling a sheet of notebook paper with thoughts and ideas. The ten-year-old student closest to me was filling her page with "I Can'ts."

"I can't kick the soccer ball past second base."

"I can't do long division with more than three numerals."

"I can't get Debbie to like me."

Her page was half full and she showed no signs of letting up. She worked on with determination and persistence.

I walked down the row glancing at students' papers. Everyone was writing sentences, describing things they couldn't do.

"I can't do ten push-ups."

"I can't hit one over the left-field fence."

"I can't eat only one cookie."

By this time, the activity engaged my curiosity, so I decided to check with the teacher to see what was going on. As I approached her, I noticed that she too was busy writing. I felt it best not to interrupt.

"I can't get John's mother to come in for a teacher conference."

"I can't get my daughter to put gas in the car."

"I can't get Alan to use words instead of fists."

Thwarted in my efforts to determine why students and teacher were dwelling on the negative instead of writing the more positive "I Can" statements, I returned to my seat and continued my observations. Students wrote for another ten minutes. Most filled their page. Some started another.

"Finish the one you're on and don't start a new one," were the instructions Donna used to signal the end of the activity. Students were then instructed to fold their papers in half and bring them to the front. When students reached the teacher's desk, they placed the "I Can't" statements into an empty shoe box.

When all the student papers were collected, Donna added hers. She put the lid on the box, tucked it under her arm, and headed out the door and down the hall. Students followed the teacher. I followed the students.

Halfway down the hall the procession stopped. Donna entered the custodian's room, rummaged around and came out with a shovel. Shovel in one hand, shoe box in the other, Donna marched the students out of the school to the farthest corner of the playground. There they began to dig...

The digging took over ten minutes because most of the fourth graders wanted a turn. When the hole approached three-feet deep, the digging ended. The box of "I Can'ts" was placed in position at the bottom of the hole and quickly covered with dirt.

Thirty-one 10- and 11-year-olds stood around the freshly dug grave site. Each had at least one page full of "I Can'ts" in the shoe box, three feet under. So did their teacher.

At this point Donna announced, "Boys and girls, please join hands and bow your heads." The students complied. They quickly formed a circle around the grave, creating a bond with their hands. They lowered their heads and waited. Donna delivered the eulogy.

"Friends, we gather today to honor the memory of 'I Can't.' While he was with us on earth, he touched the lives of everyone, some more than others. His name, unfortunately, has been spoken in every public building—schools, city halls, state capitols, and yes, even the White House.

"We have provided 'I Can't' with a final resting place and a headstone that contains his epitaph. He is survived by his brothers and sister, 'I Can,' 'I Will' and 'I'm Going to Right Away.' They are not as well known as their famous relative and are certainly not as strong and powerful yet. Perhaps someday, with your help, they will make an even bigger mark on the world.

"May 'I Can't' rest in peace and may everyone present pick up their lives and move forward in his absence. Amen."

As I listened to the eulogy I realized that these students would never forget this day. The activity was symbolic, a metaphor for life. It was a right-brain experience that would stick in the unconscious and conscious mind forever.

Writing "I Can'ts," burying them and hearing the eulogy. That was a major effort on the part of this teacher. And she wasn't done yet. At the conclusion of the eulogy she turned the students around, marched them back into the classroom and held a wake.

They celebrated the passing of "I Can't" with cookies, popcorn and fruit juices. As part of the celebration, Donna cut out a large tombstone from butcher paper. She wrote the words "I Can't" at the top and put RIP in the middle. The date was added at the bottom.

The paper tombstone hung in Donna's classroom for the remainder of the year. On those rare occasions when a student forgot and said, "I Can't," Donna simply pointed to the RIP sign. The student then remembered that "I Can't" was dead and chose to rephrase the statement.

I wasn't one of Donna's students. She was one of mine. Yet that day I learned an enduring lesson from her.

Now years later, whenever I hear the phrase, "I Can't," I see images of that fourth-grade funeral. Like the students, I remember that "I Can't" is dead.[26]

Perhaps you, like Donna's students, need to have a funeral service of your own. Make a list of all your "I Can'ts" and bury them. Write an obituary and post it in a place where you will see it often. "I Can't?" Pooh. "I can do all things through Christ who gives me strength."

••• **RECOGNIZE THE LIE:** I'm a failure.

••• **REJECT THE LIE:** That is not true.

••• **REPLACE THE LIE WITH TRUTH:**

- "I can do everything through him who gives me strength" (Philippians 4:13).

- "But we have this treasure in jars of clay to show that this all-surpassing power is from God and not from us" (2 Corinthians 4:7).

- "His divine power has given us everything we need for life and godliness through our knowledge of him who called us by his own glory and goodness" (2 Peter 1:3).

- "Now to him who is able to do immeasurably more than all we ask or imagine, according to *his power that is at work within us,* to him be glory in the church and in Christ Jesus throughout all generations, for ever and ever! Amen" (Ephesians 3:20-21, emphasis added).

- "Commit to the LORD whatever you do, and your plans will succeed" (Proverbs 16:3).

9

I Can't Forgive Myself

LIE: *I can't forgive myself.*

TRUTH: *Therefore, there is now no condemnation for those who are in Christ Jesus (Romans 8:1).*

Dear Sharon:

I just read one of your devotions on receiving grace and forgiveness. You mentioned a woman who had three abortions and how she refused to forgive herself. That really touched me because, you see, eleven years ago I had an abortion. That is the first time I ever actually put that in writing. I had gotten way off track in my walk with the Lord and was angry at Him because of an extremely hurtful situation in my life. This was something I had prayed a lot about, and I blamed God for the way things turned out. It was a very dark time in my life, and I turned away from God to live a rebellious lifestyle. During that time, I got pregnant and had an abortion. No one knew...no one.

I wish I could go back and change things. I would willingly give my life to bring this child back, but I can't. I have asked God to forgive me, and I know that God's Word says that He is "faithful to forgive my sins" and "will remember them no more," yet I can't forgive myself.

Unlike the woman in your devotion, I was a Christian when I had the abortion. I was very far from Him at the time, but I did know what I was doing was wrong. I think this is why it has been so difficult for me to accept His forgiveness. I listened to the voice of the enemy rather than the voice of God. The Holy Spirit was still trying to speak to me, but I chose not to listen. That's why I am having trouble forgiving myself. I think it is easier for someone to embrace His forgiveness when they come to Christ, but I am struggling because I already was a Christian.

How can I forgive myself?

Kimberly is not alone in her struggle to forgive herself, and her struggle has Satan's fingerprints all over it. The enemy knows that God forgave her the moment she asked. Satan can't do anything about that. But he can keep her from *feeling* forgiven. As long as she continues to feel condemned, then Satan's lie can hold her back from walking in the freedom God has so graciously given.

The Cleansing Confession

What did I tell Kimberly? I pointed her to King David. David was a man who loved the Lord with all his heart. He was anointed as the future king of Israel when he was but a young lad, killed the Philistine giant Goliath with a sling and a stone when he was but a teen, and brought the ark of the covenant back to its rightful place in Jerusalem when no one else could. But about ten years after David became established as king, during springtime when the fighting men went off to war, he decided to sit this one out. David stayed back at the palace rather than join his men on the battlefield. He wasn't where he was supposed to be, not doing what he was supposed to be doing.

One evening David decided to enjoy the cool night air and take a stroll on his flat rooftop. While glancing about, he noticed his neighbor's beautiful wife bathing. Rather than turn away, David stared at the seductive vision and wanted what he saw. David inquired and discovered that this woman was Bathsheba, wife of one of his fighting men who was off at war. He sent for her, and their night of passion conceived a child. David ordered Uriah to come home for a respite in hopes that he would sleep with his wife and believe the child was his.

But the loyal Uriah would not think of it. "The ark and Israel and Judah are staying in tents," he said, "and my master Joab and my lord's men are camped in the open fields. How could I go to my house to eat and drink and lie with my wife? As surely as you live, I will not do such a thing!" (2 Samuel 11:11).

Uriah's loyalty foiled David's cover up, so he ordered the commander of the army to put Uriah on the front lines and then withdraw, leaving him open and unprotected. Uriah was murdered just as surely as if David had put his very own sword through the soldier's heart.

I can still remember the first time I read this account. My heart broke at the thought of someone that was so close to God failing so miserably. And then I began to see just how easily it could happen to anyone...even to me.

David did not repent, but kept his sin hidden like a cancerous mass that ate away at his very soul. In Psalm 38 he wrote,

> My guilt has overwhelmed me
> like a burden too heavy to bear.
> My wounds fester and are loathsome
> because of my sinful folly
> (vv. 4-5).

Only later, when he was confronted by the prophet Nathan, did he truly confess his sin, repent, and turn back to God. And what did God do? He forgave him.

David was held in the vise grip of guilt, unsure if he could ever be set free. But mercy came with the key of forgiveness and flung the prison door open wide. David then had to take the necessary steps to walk out of the prison and into the kingdom of grace.

No matter what we have done, God does not want us to stay in the pit of guilt. "It is for freedom that Christ has set us free" (Galatians 5:1). Jesus came that we might have not only eternal life after physical death but abundant life beginning at our spiritual birth.

I in no way want to diminish the seriousness of sin. Neither do I want to lessen the truth of grace. Our sinful state before we came to Christ is the very thing that separated us from God. But when we come to God and confess our sins, the Bible promises that "he is faithful and just and will forgive us our sins and purify us from all unrighteousness" (1 John 1:9).

The Bible also goes on to say, "If we claim we have not sinned, we make him out to be a liar and his word has no place in our lives" (1 John 1:10). I haven't met anyone who honestly believes they are without sin. However, I meet people every day who believe they are without forgiveness. So let's look at these verses for a moment.

To confess is to agree with God about our sins. It is futile to think that we can keep our sins to ourselves. God already knows every move we make, every thought we think, and every word we whisper. Unconfessed sin clogs the channel through which God's power flows. Confession and repentance remove the blockage and open the pipes so the Spirit can flow freely again.

We can agree with God over our sin—confess—but still remain in darkness by refusing to accept and believe we are forgiven. As Beth Moore says, "Agreeing with God over our forgiven state is just as important as agreeing with God over our sin. If Satan can't tempt us to hide our sin and refuse to confess, he'll tempt us not to accept our forgiven and purified state. If we persist in feeling bad, we will think destructively and ultimately act on it. Don't let the devil get away with that!"[27]

To say, "I don't feel forgiven," is to allow feelings to override the truth. Truth is truth whether we believe it or not. But believing the truth will set us free. That's where the power comes from—believing God.

What does God require? "If we confess our sins, [God] is faithful and just and will forgive us our sins and purify us from all unrighteousness." Why should we require more from ourselves than our Creator requires of us?

The Real Heart of Repentance

Many people don't feel forgiven because they don't understand true repentance. Repentance means turning from our sin and toward God. It is changing our mind that leads to changing our direction.

When the religious leaders brought the woman caught in adultery to Jesus, He did not condemn her, He forgave her. But before she turned to walk away, Jesus said, "Go and sin no more." That is the key to true repentance. It is more than being sorry that I got caught. It is a deeply sincere sorrow that I have sinned against God. It is a change of the mind that in turn changes the entire person.

Joseph was a handsome, well-built young man and worked in the household of Potiphar. Potiphar's wife was attracted to the new slave boy and tried to seduce him on several occasions. "Come to bed with me," she cooed.

But Joseph said, "How could I do such a wicked thing and sin against God?" (Genesis 39:9).

Oh, that we would see our sin in such a light—not just worrying about getting caught, but being brokenhearted to think we could disappoint God.

David was a believer in God when he sinned. But God forgave him and blessed his reign. Peter was a disciple when he denied three times that he knew Jesus. But Jesus forgave him and increased his ministry. Not once will we find an example of God turning His back on someone who is truly repentant.

Many believe that simply repenting, confessing, and asking is too simple considering the wrong that was committed. They think they must serve penance or pay for their sins before they can be forgiven. But there's nothing we could ever do that would be enough to pay for our sin. No amount of penance would suffice. Nothing can wash away the stain of sin except the blood of Jesus. We can't do it. Jesus already has.

The Shadow of Shame

Two of Satan's greatest weapons against women today are shame and condemnation. Even though we know that God has forgiven us, many rise each morning to put on the familiar dirty rags. Listen to what these women said:

> In my 20s I had three abortions. I have had the hardest time forgiving myself. In my Bible study, we were talking about sexual purity. A few of the women opened up and shared that they had had an abortion. I could not share with them that I had three. I am still having a hard time forgiving myself. I know in my heart that I am forgiven, but Satan keeps a hold of my mind in this department, and I keep feeling shame. I am now married and have three children. My little girl has suffered from seizures since she was five months old, and I sometimes wonder if God is punishing me. But even as I write this, God has reminded me that it is because of her struggles I have turned back to Him and rededicated my life to Christ. My daughter is the reason for my spiritual growth. That's not a punishment, is it? That is a blessing.

* * * * *

> A while back, I had an affair. I have asked God to forgive me many times. But Satan keeps reminding me of it. I know God and my husband have both forgiven me. But I go through periods of beating myself up. I need to learn how to let it go for good.

If we are feeling condemnation, it is not coming from God. Satan condemns. The Holy Spirit convicts. How do we know the difference? Satan accuses us to make us feel condemned. The Holy Spirit convicts us to bring us to repentance (2 Corinthians 7:9-10). Once we have repented and asked for forgiveness, it is finished, over and done with, wiped away. If feelings of condemnation persist, they are a result of listening to the accusations of the enemy...listening to the lie.

Admittedly, guilt is a powerful motivator. Parents use it, employers use it, teachers use it, friends use it, kids use it, and spouses use it. But I am opposed to using guilt as a motivator because it is the very language of the enemy himself. I want to stay just as far away from Satan's native tongue as possible. When it comes to using guilt-infested words to motivate, don't speak it and don't receive it.

The feeling of not being able to forgive myself is steeped in self-loathing—anger with myself or blaming myself. Satan tries to keep us in a morbid mindset of self-loathing. It is part of his job description as "accuser of the brethren." It comes in the form of "you deserve what you got." "You made your bed now lie in it." Not only that, "You made your bed, now you stay in it."

Satan knows that the slightest whisper of guilt is easily received by a fragile heart plundered by life. Do not let the enemy convince you to stay in the prison of guilt and shame. The sentence has already been served. You are free to go.

The Freedom of Forgiveness

Here is the promise: "If we confess our sins, he is faithful and just and will forgive us our sins and purify us from all unrighteousness" (1 John 1:9). Have I said that already? Well, it deserves repeating.

God knows that many of us will still feel condemned. John wrote: "This then is how we know that we belong to the truth, and how we set our hearts at rest in his presence *whenever our hearts condemn us.* For God is greater than our hearts, and he knows everything" (1 John 3:19-20). Our hearts might condemn us, but God is greater than our hearts. We might feel condemned, but simply put, it is not true.

Our self-condemnation cannot block God's forgiveness, but it can stand as a roadblock to walking in freedom. And who holds the megaphone of condemnation? The enemy. He can do nothing to stop you from receiving God's forgiveness, but he can do much to make you feel as if you haven't. We will never be free of our past sins until we accept God's forgiveness and believe with our whole being that we are totally redeemed, completely restored, and eternally saved. The slate is wiped clean, the record expunged, and the sentence served.

Romans 5:1 states that we *have been* justified through faith. That is past tense. When Jesus said on the cross, "It is finished," He meant

His work of redemption was complete. Satan lies to us to tell us we must do more to be forgiven. So many work hard to receive something they already have and to become someone they already are.

Some engage in relentless activity to earn forgiveness. But dear friend, it will never be enough. There is only one way to "feel" forgiven and that is by accepting what Jesus did on the cross. Satan lost the battle for my soul when I was fourteen years old. And while he knows that I am forgiven and set free, his only recourse is to try to make me *feel* unforgiven and captive to my old ways.

Imagine a brand new home with beautifully placed brick, securely shingled roof, and shiny wide windows. Imagine a manicured lawn, a welcoming front door, and a sprinkling of flowers under neatly trimmed shrubs. Got the picture in your mind? Now, imagine a sign in the front yard that reads: "Posted. Condemned. Keep Out." That would be silly, wouldn't it? Of course it would.

God holds the title deed for my life and yours. The truth is that we are a brand new creation, not a condemned structure about to fall apart. Take that sign down. It really looks foolish in a heart that is beautifully crafted by the Master Builder Himself.

God's U-Turns

Dear Sharon:

Last year, I saw your book in a Christian bookstore. The title, *Your Scars Are Beautiful to God,* touched me so much my eyes filled with tears. I thought to myself, "My scars are not beautiful to God." I went home, but could not escape that title. The next day I went back and bought the book.

I am 61 years old. When I was 16, I had an abortion. I have carried those scars my whole life. I became a Christian and asked God to forgive me. I know He did, but I could not forgive myself. I continued to suffer from shame and deep sorrow. I never spoke about the abortion to anyone. It was too painful. When I brought your book home, I went into my room, shut the door, and asked

God to help me get through the pages. As I read, I could feel His healing taking place.

In the story of Joseph, I found my answer. You mentioned that Joseph had two sons. The firstborn was named Manasseh, which means "God has made me forget all my trouble and all my father's household." The second was named Ephraim, which means "God has made me fruitful in the land of my suffering." You said, "It is the same with you and with me. God does not want us to simply forget the pain of the past. He wants us to be fruitful in the land of our suffering. Use it for good. Minister to others. Plant seeds of hope."

All my life I had buried the memories and tried to forget. This had never worked. The pain did not go away. Through the names of Joseph's sons, I realized that God did not want me to forget the pain of my past, but to be fruitful in the land of my suffering and allow Him to use what I have gone through for good.

I began writing in my journal all that I was learning about healing and forgiveness. The dam over my heart broke and words began to flow onto the pages. I poured out all the things I wanted to say to my child, and I believe she heard every word. The more I wrote, the more hope and joy I felt. I knew God was helping me express my pain for the first time. There were many tears but also much joy. I asked God to help me be fruitful through this experience and told Him I was willing to use my pain for a purpose.

Satan was using the lie of unforgiveness to hold Carol back, but once she accepted the truth of God's grace, the barricade was removed and she experienced the freedom that was there all along.

What Are We Doing Here?

It has been said that 75 percent of all mentally disturbed people would be pronounced well if only they could be convinced that they are forgiven.[28] The enemy tells us that we must pay a debt that we never could. The truth tells us that God, through Jesus Christ, already has.

Imagine that you are hiding in a pitch-black, dark closet of shame. As you are crouched down on the floor, you bump into someone crouched down right beside you. You pull out a flashlight tucked in your pocket and shine the light and behold, the person in the closet with you is Jesus! When you shine the light on His face, He simply says, "Friend, what are we doing here?"

Believe the truth of God's forgiveness, embrace the truth of redemption, and come out of hiding for good. You are forgiven and free.

• • • **RECOGNIZE THE LIE:** I can't forgive myself.

• • • **REJECT THE LIE:** That is not true.

• • • **REPLACE THE LIE WITH TRUTH:**
- "If we confess our sins, he is faithful and just and will forgive us our sins and purify us from all unrighteousness" (1 John 1:9).
- "Therefore, there is now no condemnation for those who are in Christ Jesus, because through Christ Jesus the law of the Spirit of life set me free from the law of sin and death" (Romans 8:1).
- "God made him who had no sin to be sin for us, so that in him we might become the righteousness of God" (2 Corinthians 5:21).

10

I Can't Forgive the Person Who Hurt Me

LIE: *I can't forgive the person who hurt me.*

TRUTH: *I can forgive because Christ has forgiven me (Ephesians 4:32).*

Corrie Ten Boom spent many years in a German concentration camp where she was daily humiliated, degraded, and abused by Nazi guards. She still recalled piles of glasses, heaps of shoes, and the ever-present stench of human waste. She recalled the fleas, the hunger, and the smell of burning flesh coming from the incinerators. She ached at the memory of her beloved sister, Betsie, dying in her arms.

At the close of World War II, Corrie walked out of the concentration camp and into a world of ministry. She traveled around the world telling about God's grace and forgiveness through Jesus Christ. "God throws our sins into the deepest of seas," she would say. "And he puts up a sign that says, 'No fishing allowed.'"

One Sunday morning, after speaking in Munich, she noticed a heavyset, balding man in a gray overcoat approach the podium.

And as she saw the man, she pictured the uniform he used to wear—at Ravensbrück. In a rush she remembered the skull and crossbones of his visor, the pathetic piles of dresses and shoes in the middle of a large cold room, and the shame of having to walk naked in front of this man. He had been one of the cruelest guards, and now she stood face-to-face with him. Her blood seemed to freeze.

The man held out his hand. "A fine message, Fraulein," he said. "How good it is to know that, as you say, all our sins are at the bottom of the sea."

She hesitated and fumbled in her purse to avoid taking his hand.

He told her he had been a guard at Ravensbrück but had since become a Christian. He knew God had forgiven him, but he wanted Corrie's forgiveness as well.

> And I stood there—I whose sins had again and again been forgiven—and could not forgive. Betsie had died in that place— could he erase her slow terrible death simply for the asking?
>
> It could not have been many seconds that he stood there—hand held out—but to me it seemed hours as I wrestled with the most difficult thing I had ever had to do, for I had to do it—I knew that. The message that God forgives has a prior condition: that we forgive those who have injured us. "If you do not forgive men their trespasses," Jesus says, "neither will your Father in heaven forgive your trespasses."
>
> I knew it not only as a commandment of God but as a daily experience...And still I stood there with the coldness clutching my heart. But forgiveness is not an emotion—I knew that too. Forgiveness is an act of the will, and the will can function regardless of the temperature of the heart. "Jesus, help me!" I prayed silently. "I can lift my hand. I can do that much. You supply the feeling."
>
> And so woodenly, mechanically, I thrust my hand into the one stretched out to me. And as I did, an incredible thing took place. The current started in my shoulder, raced down my arm, sprang into our joined hands. And then this healing warmth seemed to flood my whole being, bringing tears to my eyes.
>
> "I forgive you, brother!" I cried. "With all my heart."[29]

Corrie set the man free, but more importantly, she set herself free.

Extending Grace

In the last chapter we looked at how God forgives us graciously and completely. Now let's look forgiveness in the face and ask, Can we extend that same grace to others?

Forgiveness is a choice. It is a decision to hand the scalpel to God and allow Him to remove the tumor of offense from the heart. The person who benefits is the one from whom the malignancy has been removed. The person being forgiven rarely knows of the healing and seldom even cares.

No one deserves forgiveness. I don't deserve it. You don't deserve it. Even the most repentant heart doesn't make it deserving. Remember, by its very definition, grace is a gift we don't deserve—it's "unmerited favor from God." We don't deserve it and can't earn it. Therefore, when we forgive, we are divinely imitating the Father. "Be quick to forgive an offense. Forgive as quickly and completely as the Master forgave you" (Colossians 3:13 MSG).

Forgiving those who have hurt or abused us is perhaps one of the most difficult aspects of healing, but without it, I believe we will never truly be free. The enemy knows its destructive potential. That's why he tells us that we can't do it. We mustn't do it. If we do, then we will somehow be letting the offender go free.

But that is a lie. We can do it. We must do it. If we do not, then *we* will never be free.

Dianne Marr, in her book, *The Reluctant Traveler,* said it well: "Unforgiveness can be likened to a parasite; it feeds on the anger and hurt of its host, finding its most satisfying nourishment in human pain. It thrives on the cycle of replayed scenes, recalled anguish, and rehashed justification for holding fast to grudges. Essentially, unforgiveness grows plump on our desire for revenge."[30]

Who do you think is pushing that rewind button on the movie screen of your mind? I believe it is the enemy who wants to keep us bound to past hurts. But friend, when we choose to forgive, God turns our pain into purpose, our hurt into hope, and our misery into ministry. No wonder the enemy trembles at the idea of a wounded soul forgiving the one who has caused her pain.

Cutting Loose

What exactly is forgiveness? The Greek word is *aphiēmi,* and it means "to let go from one's power, possession, to let go free, let escape."[31] And as Beth Moore says,

> The intent of biblical forgiveness is to cut someone loose. The word picture drawn by the Greek term for *unforgiveness* is one in which the unforgiven is roped to the back of the unforgiving. How ironic. Unforgiveness is the means by which we securely bind ourselves to that which we hate most. Therefore, the Greek meaning of *forgiveness* might best be demonstrated as the practice of cutting loose the person roped to your back.[32]

Paul wrote to the Philippians: "But one thing I do: forgetting what lies behind and reaching forward to what lies ahead, I press on toward the goal for the prize of the upward call of God in Christ Jesus" (Philippians 3:13-14 NASB). What exactly did Paul have to put behind him? What or who did Paul have to forgive? Let's take a look. He recounted the cruelties in 2 Corinthians 11:23-27.

> I have worked much harder, been in prison more frequently, been flogged more severely, and been exposed to death again and again. Five times I received from the Jews the forty lashes, minus one. Three times I was beaten with rods, once I was stoned, three times I was shipwrecked, I spent a night and a day in the open sea, I have been constantly on the move. I have been in danger from rivers, in danger from bandits, in danger from my own countrymen, in danger from Gentiles; in danger in the city, in danger in the country, in danger at sea; and in danger from false brothers. I have labored and toiled and have often gone without sleep; I have known hunger and thirst and have often gone without food; I have been cold and naked.

I think we have just discovered one of the secrets to Paul's success in ministry. He did not harbor bitterness. He did not cling to unforgiveness. He put the past behind him continually and moved forward. He forgave quickly and completely.

It is especially difficult to forgive when the people who hurt you seemingly go about life as if nothing has happened. *Don't you see the destruction,* we cry. *Don't you understand how you have shattered my life?* But with deaf ears and blind eyes, they go on with life as usual—eating, drinking, working, playing, and going to church—oblivious to the pain and anguish they've inflicted.

Yes, we forgive the act and we forgive the ignorance. As Jesus died on the cross He prayed, "Father, forgive them, for they don't know what they're doing." Can we join Jesus in that prayer, "Father, forgive _____ for he has no idea how much he has hurt me." "Father, forgive _____ for she didn't know how her words would linger."

Showing Strength

When we hold a grudge against someone, the grudge ends up holding on to us. We emotionally strap on our backs the person we choose not to forgive and lug them around wherever we go. We might not have had any control over the first offense, but we do have control over whether we are going to allow it to control or color our lives.

Forgiveness is not a sign of weakness. It is a sign of strength. Beth Moore was abused as a child and shares often about the choice to forgive:

> My breakthrough came when I realized that nothing took more divine power than forgiveness, and therefore nothing was more powerful than forgiving. You will never use your own volition—the force of your will—more dramatically than when you agree with God to start forgiving. Forgiveness is not about feeling. It's about will. No stronger force exists. Forgiveness was the force that kept Christ, by His own submission, nailed to that cross. He could have taken Himself down in a split second. He could

have called upon every arch-angel in the heavens, armed and ready. Had He said the word, the seas would have swallowed the earth in one gulp.

Forgiveness is not passivity, dear one. It is power. It is the ability to withstand the pressing, quaking gates of hell. Take this power and wield it. It's your right as a child of God. In the power of Jesus, first you will it and soon you'll feel it. Start today. Confirm it tomorrow. And keep confirming it by faith as the will of God for you in Christ Jesus until you walk it by sight.[33]

But he doesn't deserve to be forgiven, I hear you say. Neither did I. Neither did you. Forgiveness has absolutely nothing to do with whether the person who hurt us deserves to be forgiven. Forgiveness is not saying that what the person did or did not do was right. It is simply saying that we are taking the person off our hook and placing them on God's hook. We are cutting them loose from our back and giving the burden to God. We are no longer allowing them to hold us captive by holding a grudge.

As long as we do not forgive, we are held in Satan's trap. It's the number one avenue by which Satan ensnares his prey. Paul wrote, "Get rid of all bitterness, rage and anger, brawling and slander, along with every form of malice" (Ephesians 4:31). Why? "In order that Satan might not outwit us. For we are not unaware of his schemes" (2 Corinthians 2:11).

Nothing will make us more bitter than an unforgiving spirit. And nothing will dissolve bitterness quicker than a decision to forgive and let go of the offense or disappointment. We cannot be bitter and get better at the same time.

Forgiveness is not

- saying that what the person did was not wrong
- absolving the person from responsibility for his actions
- denying the wrong occurred
- pretending the abuse did not happen

Forgiveness is

- letting go of your need for revenge
- cutting the person loose
- refusing to let bitterness and hatred rule your life
- leaving the past behind by not allowing it to control your actions or emotions

Six Steps to Forgiveness

Forgiveness is hard work. So is mining for gold or unearthing hidden treasure. But in the end, the valuable jewel is worth the effort. Let me walk with you through six steps to forgiveness that might help you.

1. On a piece of paper, write the name of the person who hurt you.

2. Write down how the person hurt you (rape, verbal abuse, sexual abuse, neglect, betrayal, desertion, rejection).

3. Write down how you feel about that person. Be honest. God knows how you feel.

4. Decide to forgive. Forgiveness is not a feeling but a decision of the will. God will never tell us to do something without providing the power to obey. He has told us to forgive and will give us the power to do so—but it all begins with the decision to do so.

5. Take your list to God and confess your forgiveness to Him. "Lord, I come to You today and give up my unforgiveness. I forgive _____ for _____ . At this moment, I choose not to hold his/her offense against him/her, but put them into your hands. I pray that you will heal my emotional wounds and help me to be able to help someone else with the same comfort you have given me. I cut _____ loose."

6. As a visual exercise, destroy the list. Some have taken the list to a

fireplace and burned it. Others have actually nailed the paper to a wooden cross. Still others have written the name of the person they are forgiving on a helium balloon and released it to heaven. However you choose, give the name to God.[34]

Beth Set Free

When Beth was ten years old, she was raped by James, a neighborhood boy. Beth's little heart was so battered and bruised that she transferred her hatred to all men and looked on them with disdain. It seemed as if this boy's face was on every man she saw, and none were to be trusted. She bore a fear that she would be raped again, and that terror stifled her relationships with men.

At a women's retreat where I spoke about the freedom of forgiveness, Beth made a decision to cut James loose. Did she feel like it? No. She simply made a decision that she was not going to let the rape control her any longer, and forgiveness was the only way. Did he deserve to be forgiven? No, but she deserved to be free. It had nothing to do with him and everything to do with her. So she gave the offender to God—took him off her hook and placed him on God's. She felt somewhat better, but the true test was yet to come.

Several months later, Beth and her mother decided to have a yard sale. Her mother invited her neighbor to join them and pool their wares. This happened to be James' parents, though they didn't know about the rape. It had been Beth's well-kept secret. While they were categorizing and pricing their items, James called.

"Hey, Mom," he said. "I went to your house and you weren't there, so I thought I'd try the Smiths'" (not their real name).

"Yeah, we're here getting ready for a yard sale tomorrow," she said. "Come on over."

For a second, Beth didn't know what to do. An urge to run bubbled up within her. *By the grace of God I am not going to let this control me any longer,* she silently prayed. *I am healed and set free, and there is nothing he can do to take that away from me unless I let him.*

When James came into the room, Beth smiled and said, "Hi, James. How are you?"

James was wearing a lewd t-shirt with an image of a girl pole dancing on the front. He refused to make eye contact with Beth. She wondered if he was ashamed. Now he was the one held captive by his actions.

"*Before* I became a Christian," Beth explained, "I would have lectured him on women's rights and used a lot of four-letter words. Then I would have gone in the house and cried. I would have cut myself because that was the only way I knew how to cope with the pain and shame of the rape. *After* I became a Christian, I probably would have been able to keep my mouth shut and prayed instead of cutting myself, but I certainly would have cried about it for days. But this time, it didn't even hurt. I was able to feel compassion for him. He's just lost like I was before I came to Christ, and I'm certain that I, just like him, left a trail of hurting people in my wake.

"It was at that very moment, standing among the clutter of the yard sale items, that I realized God had cleaned the clutter from my heart. I was totally healed. God had set me completely free from fear and anxiety over being raped again. Now I walk with courage and bravery into my past rather than pushing the feelings down and pretending they're not there. I am confident that He who began a great work in me is faithful to finish it!"

Someone once said, "We are most like beasts when we kill. We are most like men when we judge. We are most like God when we forgive."

● ● ● **RECOGNIZE THE LIE**: I can't forgive the person who hurt me.

● ● ● **REJECT THE LIE**: That is not true.

● ● ● **REPLACE THE LIE WITH TRUTH**:

  • "Then Peter came and said to Him, 'Lord, how often shall my brother sin against me and I forgive him? Up to seven times?'

Jesus said to him, 'I do not say to you, up to seven times, but up to seventy times seven'" (Matthew 18:21-22 NASB).

• "Bear with each other and forgive whatever grievances you may have against one another. Forgive as the Lord forgave you" (Colossians 3:13).

• "Be kind and compassionate to one another, forgiving each other, just as in Christ God forgave you" (Ephesians 4:32).

11

I Would Be Happy If

Lie: *I would be happy if* _____.

Truth: *My joy comes from the Lord (Psalm 126:3).*

Do you want to hold her?" Karen asked.

I couldn't see the infant in question. Her mother had her wrapped up like a child about to enter a blizzard, though the room was warmed by the heat of fifty women and a table full of crock pots and casseroles. I couldn't see her, but I knew that somewhere in the depths of that pink, fleecy cloth, little Makenna Purdue waited. At least five other women had held her already, and now it was my turn.

I was forty-one years old and I'd never conceived a child of my own. I'd never rested my hand on my stomach in awe of the life growing inside. I'd never had the privilege of bringing a minia-ture clone of myself to a Bible-study potluck and offering peeks and cuddles to my friends. So the question remained: Did I want to hold another woman's baby?[35]

As I read the words from my friend, Shannon Woodward, I under-stood exactly how she felt. I can still remember the day when the word *infertile* was written on my medical chart. An emptiness I had never experienced before echoed in my hollow heart. *What have I done wrong? Why is God punishing me? Am I not worthy to raise another human being?* I prayed, repented of everything I could think of, fasted, and begged God to intervene. I changed my diet, had two exploratory surgeries, injected and ingested hormones, and had timed intimate relations with my husband (which is anything but intimate). I was determined to outsmart the diagnosis.

But it didn't happen, and I understood the pain of empty arms and missing someone I'd never met. Our five-bedroom dream house was a daily reminder of beds that would not be slept in, toys that would not be scattered, and children that would not be tucked in beds at night.

Steve and I do have one amazing son. Steven Hugh Jaynes Jr. was born on a frosty February morning, and I never knew so much love could be wrapped in one tiny package. But God closed my womb for the possibility of siblings for him. Steven was conceived with no trouble whatsoever, and we were surprised and brokenhearted when we learned he would be our only child. But through the painful years of infertility, God unfolded a plan, a purpose, and a promise. He began to show me just what I needed to be happy…Him.

The Lie in the Garden

The lie "I would be happy if _____ " is really nothing new, is it? It's the same lie the serpent whispered to Eve. *You would be happy if you eat the forbidden fruit.* Today, he hisses the same worm-ridden lies.

- I would be happy if I had a child.
- I would be happy if I had two children.
- I would be happy if I had a husband.
- I would be happy if my husband treated me better.
- I would be happy if I had a different husband.
- I would be happy if I had more money.
- I would be happy if I had a better job.
- I would be happy if…

I could fill the rest of this book with "I would be happy ifs." But here's the truth. Our ultimate happiness will be found only in Jesus Christ. We can't explore all the lies of "I would be happy if," but let's look at just a few.

I Would be Happy if I Had Children

In the Bible, Sarah was so distraught that she did not have a child that she convinced her husband, Abram, to father a child by sleeping with her maid. Was she happy when the child was placed in her arms? No, she was so jealous over Hagar, she stormed into Abram's office and demanded that he send both Hagar and the child away.

Then there was Elizabeth, Zechariah's wife. She was well up in years and had never had a child. I'm sure she had days when her heart ached at the sound of a baby's cry wafting through the neighborhood. I imagine she wiped away a few tears when she passed mothers with children in tow at the market. But it seems she had a full life with her husband the priest. God did eventually bless her with a son in her later years, but she seemed content before.

I think of Esther, a Jewish orphan beauty married to a Gentile king. We never read about Esther having children, but we do marvel at how she saved an entire Hebrew nation from extinction. Purpose? She had purpose.

I think of Anna—a widowed woman who spent almost her entire adult life praying and fasting in the temple, waiting for the arrival of the promised Messiah. She was one of a handful of people to whom God chose to reveal Jesus' true identity at his birth. Fulfilment? She had fulfillment.

Many incredibly godly women in the Bible experienced infertility: Sarah, Elizabeth, Hannah, Rachel, just to name a few. Luke tells us Elizabeth and her husband were "upright in the sight of God, observing all the Lord's commandments and regulations blamelessly. But they had no children, because Elizabeth was barren; and they were both well along in years" (Luke 1:6-7). Infertility was not God's punishment, but His plan.

Yes, God has fashioned a woman's body and her heart to bear and nurture children. But if He chooses for a woman not to bear children, that doesn't mean she will not be fulfilled nor have a wonderful purposeful life. However, the enemy can scream about what we do not have in order to mask the gentle whisper of God that reminds us of what we do.

One day, as I was studying the Song of Solomon, I was struck with verse one of chapter two. I was reading it as if Jesus was the groom and I was his beloved bride (which I am). The bride said, "I am a rose of Sharon."

God stopped me. *What is your name?* He seemed to say.

My name is Sharon, I replied.

Go look it up, He prompted.

When I looked up *Sharon* in my Bible dictionary, I discovered that it meant "a fertile valley." Then God began to reveal His plan for me. Even though my medical chart said, "Infertile," He made sure my name was Sharon—"fertile valley." And while my dream to have a house full of children with Jaynes blood coursing through their veins did not happen the way I had dreamed, God fulfilled my dreams by giving me a passel of spiritual children all around the world.

> He settles the barren woman in her home
>   as a happy mother of children.
> Praise the LORD
>   (Psalm 113:9).

Having children is not the ultimate source of happiness and joy. Being smack dab in the middle of God's will is.

I Would Be Happy if I Were Married (or if I Were Married to a Different Man)

I dare say that more than half of the e-mails I receive asking for prayer are about marriage difficulties. Single women long to be married, married women want to be single, and some just want to trade in their husbands for a different model. Marriage is not the key to happiness.

Dick and Jane walk out of the church arm-in-arm with rice flying overhead. Tin cans tied to their car clatter in the background as they ride off into the sunset. But the next day, the sun rises again. Dick isn't prepared for mood swings, weight gain, frozen dinners, and shopping sprees. His visions of passionate sex are replaced by an obligatory three times a month at best. *She has deceived me,* he decides. *This is not what I signed up for.*

Jane is surprised by dirty socks on the floor, hours of sports TV, the dripping faucet that still isn't fixed, and the lack of romance. *All he ever thinks about is sex,* she inwardly complains. *He's lazy and irresponsible. He has deceived me. This is not what I signed up for.*

Unmet expectations are the beginning to disillusionment in any marriage. Whenever we expect someone else to make us happy, we are setting ourselves up for disappointment. That picnic will always get rained on. Other people will always disappoint us. Even a good husband makes a poor God. Other people are not meant to be our ultimate source of happiness...only God is.

Hollywood tells us that we will be happy when we find the right person. However, I have discovered that a successful marriage occurs when we *become* the right person. "For years I prayed that God would change my husband," Denise told me. "Our marriage went from bad to worse, and we ended up separated and headed for divorce. Then I began to read about what it meant to be a godly wife. In the world's eyes I was doing a pretty good job. In God's eyes I was missing the mark. So I began to pray—this time for my own heart. God gave me the answer to my prayer to change my husband...He changed me."

Unless I've missed something, I haven't found a verse yet that says God's ultimate goal for our lives is happiness. God's ultimate goal for us is conformity to the image of Christ. Many times He uses marriage as the means to bring about that change. Marriage is the art studio in which masterpieces are created. If we run out the door when the dark brushstrokes of life streak the canvas, then the beautiful reds, yellows, and greens will never have a chance to radiate on the dark background of life experiences.

In the Bible, God describes the marriage of a man and a woman as a visual example of the spiritual union between Jesus Christ and the church (all Christians). Believers are called "the bride of Christ"

(Revelation 19:7). Marriages are walking, talking, earthly examples of the heavenly relationship between God's Son and those who believe on His name. God instructs men, "Love your wives, just as Christ loved the church and gave himself up for her" (Ephesians 5:25).

Of course the enemy wants to destroy this living example. Why wouldn't he? Jesus said, "The thief [Satan] comes only to steal and kill and destroy" (John 10:10). He desires to destroy the God-ordained and designed institution of marriage. The enemy began with Adam and Eve in the Garden of Eden and continues his destructive tactics even today: temptation, control, stubbornness, and pride. Satan has proclaimed an all out assault on the family, and he begins at the top—with the husband and wife.

So many times we fail to see the real enemy in our marital struggles. As we've already seen, Paul wrote to the Ephesians, "For our struggle is not against flesh and blood, but against the rulers, against the authorities, against the powers of this dark world and against the spiritual forces of evil in the heavenly realms" (Ephesians 6:12). When I'm having a conflict with my husband, I need to stop, take a deep breath, and think, *Who is the real enemy here?* There is a spiritual battle raging all around us that we can't even see. We don't need to be afraid of the battle, but aware of the enemy's tactics.

Here's a statistic I want you to ponder: According to an analysis of the National Survey of Families and Households, 86 percent of unhappily married people who stick it out find that, five years later, their marriages are happier. Nearly 60 percent of those who rated their marriage as unhappy in the late 1980s, and who stayed married, rated that same marriage "very happy" or "quite happy" when reinterviewed five years later.[36] In comparison, those who divorced and remarried divorced again at a rate of 60 percent.[37]

So, starting over may very well be the answer to a difficult marriage...as long as it's with the same man.

Being married is not the ultimate source for happiness and joy. Being smack dab in the middle of God's will is.

I Would Be Happy if I Had More Money

My husband loves golf, and when a salesman invited him to be his guest on one of Charlotte's most prestigious courses, Steve jumped at the chance. As they drove their cart up to the sixth tee, Steve took in the tree-lined fairway dressed in pink, purple, and fuchsia azaleas in full bloom. Six multimillion dollar mansions surrounded the green. Swimming pools sat motionless, manicured lawns lay weedless, and $50,000 cars were parked in the driveways. Then Steve's host began to unfold the stories behind those walls.

"See that first house? Those folks are separated. The wife had two affairs, and her husband finally left. And that second house? The wife has caught her husband with a prostitute twice. She wants to divorce him, but she's recently inherited ten million dollars from her father and doesn't want her husband to get any of the money. She's trying to figure out the best way to get out of the marriage and keep her money.

"And that third house, the one with the yard that looks somewhat unkempt? That couple also got a divorce, and their house has been for sale for seven months." (Yes, the guy was gossiping. Not just a problem with the fairer sex.)

Steve was struck with the broken lives surrounding him. Later he told me, "These were people who had achieved everything they thought would ever make them happy, and they were miserable."

"Do you think they wanted more?" I asked.

"No, I think they wanted something different, but they don't even know what that *different* is."

David Myers, in his book *The American Paradox: Spiritual Hunger in an Age of Plenty,* notes that since 1960, the divorce rate has doubled, the teen suicide rate tripled, the violent crime rate quadrupled, and the prison population quintupled. There are increased rates of depression, anxiety, and other mental-health problems.[38] As a nation, we are three times richer than we were in 1950, but no happier. We give lip service to the old adage, "Money can't buy happiness," but we buy into the lie that it can.

Eric Weiner describes the relationship between money and happiness:

> Recent research into happiness, or subjective well-being, reveals that money does indeed buy happiness. Up to a point. That point, though, is surprisingly low: about fifteen thousand dollars a year. After that, the link between economic growth and happiness evaporates. Americans are on average three times wealthier than we were a half a century ago, yet we are no happier. The same is true of Japan and many other industrialized nations. Think about it as Richard Layard, a professor at the London School of Economics, has, "They have become richer, they work much less, they have longer holidays, they travel more, they live longer, and they are healthier. But they are no happier."[39]

One of the wealthiest men in the Bible, King Solomon, concluded that the accumulation of wealth doesn't lead to contentment ("I have seen all the things that are done under the sun; all of them are meaningless, a chasing after the wind"—Ecclesiastes 1:14), nor does the pursuit of happiness apart from God ("The eye never has enough of seeing, nor the ear its fill of hearing"—1:8). Those who seek to find their happiness in the accumulation of things will never get enough. "Remember your Creator," he concludes (12:1). That's the key. A personal relationship with the Creator is the only true source of joy. Everything else is icing on the cake.

Money will buy a lot of stuff, but it will not buy happiness. Being wealthy is not the ultimate source of happiness and joy. Being smack dab in the middle of God's will is.

The Pursuit of Happiness

So what do we really need to be happy? A man? A new house? Children? Financial security? A slimmer body? A wrinkle-free face? A new car? A fulfilling job? Successful adult children? Loving parents? Encouraging friends? A padded savings account? Good health?

We have only to look at the latest edition of *National Enquirer,*

People, or *Entertainment Tonight* to know that some of the most unhappy people on the planet are seemingly the most successful. They seem to have it all while in reality they have nothing at all.

Friend, we will never find true happiness until the only word that fills in that blank is the name of Jesus. Don't be fooled. This is the truth.

Someone asked a very wealthy man just how much it would take for him to be happy.

"Just a little bit more," he said.

But the little bit more will not satisfy the soul. Joy comes only from knowing Christ. We are each born with a God-shaped void in our lives. A husband, a child, a car, a family—nothing, absolutely nothing can fill that void successfully. There will always be emptiness surrounding the thing or person we attempt to put in the God-shape void in our lives.

Happiness won't be found by investing in the stock market but by investing in people. It won't be found by spending money but by spending time with family and friends. It won't be found by getting but by giving. The Declaration of Independence declares the right to pursue happiness, but it fails to give the guidelines to make that possible.

Like trying to read a crumpled map in a glove compartment, we try to find the way to happiness. We hold the creased pages that have been taped together and run our finger along the highway, looking for shortcuts. Jesus said, "I am the way and the truth and the life" (John 14:6). He is the highway to holiness, the roadway to righteousness, and the pathway to peace.

Every year, nearly forty million Americans move. Some moves are work related, health related, or relationship related. But mostly, people move because they think they will be happier somewhere else.

The truth is, as long as we live in this world, we will never be completely content. We are not made for this world. We were made for heaven. C.S. Lewis said, "If I find in myself a desire which no experience in this world can satisfy, the most probable explanation is that I was made for another world."

We were made for heaven. This world is temporary and fleeting...just a breath. We are homesick, in a way, for a place we've never been.

But God does give us glimpses of home. Every time we spend time in His presence, we get a glimpse of our heavenly home, a taste of our eternal life, and an inkling of our everlasting peace. Wow, I can't wait.

There Is No Other Stream

In *The Silver Chair,* the fourth book in the Chronicles of Narnia, C.S. Lewis introduces a new character to the land of Narnia. Jill finds herself transported to Narnia as if she were caught up in a dream. The first creature she encounters is Aslan the lion, the Christ figure throughout the series. Aslan appears for a moment, then stalks slowly back into the forest. Jill is terribly afraid of meeting up with the lion, but her increasing thirst drives her in search for water. Alas! Jill discovers a stream, but she has to pass Aslan to reach it.

> "Are you not thirsty?" said the Lion.
>
> "I'm dying of thirst," said Jill.
>
> "Then drink," said the Lion.
>
> "May I—could I—would you mind going away while I do?" said Jill.
>
> The Lion answered this only by a look and a very low growl. And as Jill gazed at its motionless bulk, she realized that she might as well have asked the whole mountain to move aside for her convenience.
>
> The delicious rippling noise of the stream was driving her nearly frantic.
>
> "Will you promise not to—do anything to me, if I do come?" said Jill.
>
> "I make no promise," said the Lion.
>
> Jill was so thirsty now that, without noticing it, she had come a step nearer.

"Do you eat girls?" she said.

"I have swallowed up girls and boys, women and men, kings and emperors, cities and realms," said the Lion. It didn't say this as if it were boasting, nor as if it were sorry, nor as if it were angry. It just said it.

"I daren't come and drink," said Jill.

"Then you will die of thirst," said the Lion.

"Oh dear!" said Jill, coming another step nearer. "I suppose I must go and look for another stream then."

"There is no other stream," said the Lion.[40]

Friend, there is no other stream that will quench our thirst. Neither people, nor places, nor possessions will satisfy that longing. Only Jesus…He is the living water, the bread of life, the lover of our soul.

••• **RECOGNIZE THE LIE:** I would be happy if _____.

••• **REJECT THE LIE:** That is not true.

••• **REPLACE THE LIE WITH TRUTH:**

- "I have learned to be content whatever the circumstances. I know what it is to be in need, and I know what it is to have plenty. I have learned the secret of being content in any and every situation, whether well fed or hungry, whether living in plenty or in want. I can do everything through him who gives me strength" (Philippians 4:11-13).

- "I have set the LORD always before me. Because he is at my right hand, I will not be shaken. Therefore my heart is glad and my tongue rejoices; my body also will rest secure" (Psalm 16:8-9).

- "The LORD is my shepherd; I have all that I need" (Psalm 23:1 NLT).

12

I Can't Help Myself

LIE: *I can't help myself.*

TRUTH: *I am more than a conqueror through Christ Jesus, my Lord (Romans 8:37).*

One spring, Mr. and Mrs. Cottontail decided to start their family under our backyard gazebo, but not everyone in the Jaynes family was happy with the situation. Ginger, our golden retriever, wanted them gone. Several times I caught her pawing at the dirt around the gazebo trying her best to get to them.

"No, Ginger," I said. "Get away from there!"

After being away for a weekend, we drove up the driveway to see the beautifully landscaped gazebo standing naked. Ginger had dug up all the bushes, flowers, and pine straw, and the gazebo's once-hidden cinderblock supports were totally exposed.

"Ginger, you are a bad dog," I said. "Look at what you've done!"

She tucked her tail between her legs and slunk back into the garage. I'm not sure she understood what she had done, but she did understand that we were not happy.

Steve spent hours replanting the bushes and flowers. All the while, little bunnies snuck a peek at this human repairing the circumference of their home. One brave bunny ventured out from his safe haven. Quicker than you could say "jackrabbit," Ginger grabbed the unsuspecting rabbit in her mouth.

"Steve, Ginger's got a bunny!" I said.

Steve grabbed Ginger by the collar and gently removed the bunny from her mouth. "I think she broke its legs," he said.

"I am so mad at Ginger," I said. "I'm not sure I want a dog that would hurt a bunny."

"Sharon, you can't get mad at a dog for acting like a dog."

Steve was right. I can't get mad at a dog for acting like a dog. That's just what they do—especially a retriever. Unfortunately, many Christians have that same attitude. "I just can't help myself," they say. "This is just the way I am." But friend, if you know Jesus Christ as your Savior, then you have the power of the Holy Spirit living in you. No, you cannot help yourself on your own strength, but the Holy Spirit is more than able to help you if you call on him.

A New Creation

The truth is, you are a new creation in Christ (2 Corinthians 5:17). Before we come to Christ, we really can't help ourselves. Oh sure, we can make positive decisions and choose to act properly. But the power to overcome sin is not present. As the apostle Paul said,

> The mind of sinful man is death, but the mind controlled by the Spirit is life and peace; the sinful mind is hostile to God. It does not submit to God's law, nor can it do so. Those controlled by the sinful nature cannot please God.
>
> You, however, are controlled not by the sinful nature but by the Spirit, if the Spirit of God lives in you. And if anyone does not have the Spirit of Christ, he does not belong to Christ (Romans 8:6-8).

When Paul refers to the "sinful mind," he is speaking of the mind of a person who is not a new creation in Christ. Once we come to Christ, we can no longer truthfully say, "I can't help myself. This is just the way I am." The truth is, "That's just the way I was. I now have the power of the Holy Spirit living in me. I can do all things through

Christ who gives me strength. I am no longer a slave to sin. I don't have to sin. I now have a choice."

Jennifer stood in front of the mirror staring at the overweight woman looking back at her. Just two years ago she had lost 120 pounds, and now 80 of them were back. *I can't keep this weight off,* she thought. *I know what I'm supposed to do, but I just can't do it. I'm always going to be fat. I'm just going to accept it and quit trying. What's so bad about being fat anyway? I just can't help myself.*

Rachel loved Travis, she really did. Though they were both Christians, they found themselves staring at the ceiling in her bedroom after a night of passion that led to a morning of regret. *We've tried to remain pure, but we love each other so much. It's just natural to feel this passionately about the man you love. Once we start kissing, we can't stop. But I know it's wrong. I feel sick to my stomach every time we have sex. I just can't help myself.*

Martha could hear her six-year-old son crying in the next room. She was crying too. Her words of anger yelled at the top of her lungs just moments before bounced off the walls of their home. *Oh, God,* Martha prayed, *why can't I control my anger? Why can't I control the words that come out of my mouth? I am destroying my family with my words. I've tried to control my tongue, but poison seems to come out anyway. What's wrong with me? I just can't help myself.*

Paul faced this same dilemma and records his struggle in his letter to the church at Rome:

> But I need something more! For if I know the law but still can't keep it, and if the power of sin within me keeps sabotaging my best intentions, I obviously need help! I realize that I don't have what it takes. I can will it, but I can't do it. I decide to do good, but I don't really do it; I decide not to do bad, but then I do it anyway. My decisions, such as they are, don't result in actions. Something has gone wrong deep within me and gets the better of me every time.
>
> It happens so regularly that it's predictable. The moment I decide

to do good, sin is there to trip me up. I truly delight in God's commands, but it's pretty obvious that not all of me joins in that delight. Parts of me covertly rebel, and just when I least expect it, they take charge.

I've tried everything and nothing helps. I'm at the end of my rope. Is there no one who can do anything for me? Isn't that the real question? (Romans 7:17-24 MSG).

Do you sense Paul's struggle as he cries out, "Oh, what a miserable person I am! Who will free me from this life that is dominated by sin and death?" (7:24 NLT). Have you been right there with him when the wanting and the doing seem miles apart? Paul asked the question, "Is there no one who can do anything for me?" He asked the question then excitedly tells us the answer: "Thank God! The answer is in Jesus Christ our Lord" (7:25 NLT).

"I can't help myself" is a lie. Through Jesus Christ, the Anointed One, we do have the power to resist temptation and to change.

Telling Ourselves the Truth

Let's go back up to the three friends we just met and look again at their struggles. What is the truth of their situation and how can they change the messages they're telling themselves?

Jennifer: *It's silly to think that I cannot lose weight. Of course I can. I can stop buying potato chips and cookies. I can order salads at fast-food restaurants instead of hamburgers and French fries, and I can start walking every day again. I can do it. I've done it before. My body is the temple of God, and I need to take better care of it. I can do all things through Christ who gives me strength.*

Rachel: *It's ridiculous to think that I cannot control my passion with Travis. We didn't all of a sudden end up in bed. It took many steps to get here. The kiss, the touches, the walk from the den to the bedroom. We can stop this. God, I repent right now of this sin in my life. I dedicate my body to You and pray that You give me the strength to resist temptation. I will guard my heart and stop putting myself in a position to fail. I can do all things through Christ who gives me strength.*

Martha: *It's foolish to think that I cannot change the way I speak to my family. I will start each day dedicating my words to God. Set a guard over my mouth, O LORD; keep watch over the door of my lips. May the words of my mouth and the meditation of my heart be pleasing in your sight. I can do all things through Christ who gives me strength.*

When we tell ourselves that we can't help ourselves—that's just the way we are—then we see ourselves as victims. As long as we see ourselves as victims, being controlled by someone or something else, we will never change. But when we see ourselves as choice makers, we can ask God to give us the power and determination to resist temptation.

Satan knows that if he can convince us that we can't help ourselves, we will remain in bondage to the lie. The truth is, I can choose to believe differently, and by the power of the Holy Spirit living in me, I can choose to act differently. Choice. Free will. God took a great risk when he gave man free will. It is a blessing and a curse. How we engage that free will determines which.

There is always a choice. The world teaches that we have no control over many sinful behaviors. "I was born this way." Born this way? Yes, we are born bent toward sin, but we are not born genetically disposed to a lifestyle of sin that we have no control over. When tempted, a believer has a choice to respond according to the flesh or according to the Spirit (the power of God working in us). These two are in opposition to one another (Galatians 5:17).

Continuing to walk in a particular sin will lead to the development of a stronghold in your life, a negative way of thinking that is built brick by brick, thought by repetitious thought, over time or by a one-time traumatic event. The next thing you know, a person living in a stronghold is thinking, "I can't help myself," whereas she or he most definitely can call on the power of God to blast the walls of the stronghold apart. We have "divine power to demolish strongholds" (2 Corinthians 10:4).

From my earliest remembrance, I entertained thoughts of inadequacy. I always felt that I wasn't good enough. No one had any idea

I was in bondage to this stronghold because "we try harder" was the inner voice that drove me. No one saw the invisible ball and chain I carried around everywhere I went. I drug the chains right along with me on the cheerleading squad for six years, across the stage to receive my induction into the National Honor Society, and into one of the best universities in our state.

Until I accepted Christ, I was an insecure nonbeliever. After I came to Christ, I became an insecure believer. Oh sure, I read the verse that said I was a new creation in Christ, but I had no idea what that meant. As far as I knew, I now had my "get out of hell free" card, but I didn't think I was good enough to make any lasting impact while here on earth. "We try harder" became my spiritual mantra.

See, I was trying to "help myself" rather than relying on the power of the Holy Spirit to work through me and in me. In my flesh, on my own power, I can't help myself. But through the power of the Holy Spirit, I can do all things through Christ who strengthens me.

As we recognize the lies that have been programmed into our minds, reject those lies, and replace those lies with truth, we will begin to break down the stronghold of "I can't help myself." The flag of inadequacy will come down from the castle of our hearts and a new flag of confidence will be raised.

Embracing the Promise, Purpose, and Power of the Holy Spirit

If you were going off to war and knew that you were going to be put on the front lines and probably would not be coming back home to your family, what would you tell them? Think of the final instructions you would give your children, the affirmation of your love you would whisper to your spouse, and the words of endearment you would share with your friends.

Jesus was in that very situation as He shared His last meal with the disciples in the upper room. All along, Jesus had given them clues about how His earthly life would end and the purpose for His brief life here on earth. But they did not understand. They refused to believe that their king would be anything other than worshipped as He had been when He rode into town on the back of a donkey and was hailed with palm branches and praise.

During their last meal together, I imagine Jesus went through a mental list of what He needed to tell His friends before He went to the cross. John records those precious moments in John 13–17. Those words are some of the most endearing of Scripture and ones that I read time and time again. I encourage you to read those chapters and place yourself in that room with Jesus, for you, dear one, are one of His disciples, and the words Jesus shared with the Twelve are meant for you as well.

Let's look at one particular word of comfort and instruction regarding a special parting gift that Jesus was leaving his trusted friends. Jesus said:

> "I tell you the truth, anyone who has faith in me will do what I have been doing. He will do even greater things than these, because I am going to the Father. And I will do whatever you ask in my name, so that the Son may bring glory to the Father. You may ask me for anything in my name, and I will do it.

> "If you love me, you will obey what I command. And I will ask the Father, and he will give you another Counselor to be with you forever—the Spirit of truth. The world cannot accept him, because it neither sees him nor knows him. But you know him, for he lives with you and will be in you. I will not leave you as orphans; I will come to you. Before long, the world will not see me anymore, but you will see me. Because I live, you also will live. On that day you will realize that I am in my Father, and you are in me, and I am in you. Whoever has my commands and obeys them, he is the one who loves me. He who loves me will be loved by my Father, and I too will love him and show myself to him" (John 14:12-21).

Did you catch that the Holy Spirit had been *with* them, but now He was going to be *in* them? What difference do you think that would make in someone's life? What difference has that made in your life?

Jesus gave them the promise of the Holy Spirit, and then He told them the purpose of the Holy Spirit.

> "But I tell you the truth: It is for your good that I am going away. Unless I go away, the Counselor will not come to you; but if I go, I will send him to you...
>
> "I have much more to say to you, more than you can now bear. But when he, the Spirit of truth, comes, he will guide you into all truth. He will not speak on his own; he will speak only what he hears, and he will tell you what is yet to come. He will bring glory to me by taking from what is mine and making it known to you. All that belongs to the Father is mine. That is why I said the Spirit will take from what is mine and make it known to you" (John 16:7, 12-15).

Once again, after Jesus' death and resurrection, He left the disciples with final instructions before taking His seat at the right hand of God in paradise...and it involved the Holy Spirit. He had given them the promise and the purpose, now He told them to wait for the power.

> "Do not leave Jerusalem, but wait for the gift my Father promised, which you have heard me speak about. For John baptized with water, but in a few days you will be baptized with the Holy Spirit...But you will receive power when the Holy Spirit comes on you; and you will be my witnesses in Jerusalem, and in all Judea and Samaria, and to the ends of the earth" (Acts 1:4-5,8).

A few days later, the Holy Spirit fell on the disciples and transformed a bunch of bungling cowards into powerful prophesying preachers. They commanded the lame to walk, cast out demons, preached to the masses, confronted angry crowds, and laughed in the face of death.

They changed the world.

Since that glorious day at Pentecost, when the Holy Spirit fell on the worshipping believers, a new day was unleashed for the church. The Holy Spirit now resides in every person who has accepted Jesus as Lord and Savior (Romans 8:9). The Spirit of the living God has empowered us with the same power that raised Jesus from the dead.

Then why don't we exercise that power? Because we don't believe.

In third-world countries, it is not unusual to hear of miraculous healings, signs, and wonders, and even the raising of the dead. No one told them that those things don't happen anymore. Praise God for that! They believe in the power of the Holy Spirit in their lives and expect God to show up when they call on His name. Oh that we would put our sophisticated, over-educated minds aside and come to God as children who believe He is who He says He is and does what He says He will do.

When we come to Christ, we are given the Holy Spirit as a deposit of our heavenly inheritance (Ephesians 1:14), as a seal upon our hearts (Ephesians 1:13), and as a permanent resident within us (Hebrews 13:5). But we have the choice to cooperate with Him and walk in victory or ignore Him and stumble in defeat.

"I can't help myself?" Hogwash, as my country grandmother would say. God has given us the power to do everything He has called us to do—and that includes living a life of obedience. It is a lie of the enemy that says "I can't help myself." It is the truth of God that says, "I can do everything through him who gives me strength" (Philippians 4:13).

••• **RECOGNIZE THE LIE:** I can't help myself.

••• **REJECT THE LIE:** That's not true.

••• **REPLACE THE LIE WITH TRUTH:**
  • "You have been set free from sin and have become slaves to righteousness...Through Christ Jesus the law of the Spirit of life set me free from the law of sin and death" (Romans 6:18; 8:2).

  • "God is faithful; he will not let you be tempted beyond what you can bear. But when you are tempted, he will also provide a way out so that you can stand up under it" (1 Corinthians 10:13).

  • "His divine power has given us everything we need for life and godliness through our knowledge of him who called us by his own glory and goodness. Through these he has given us his very great and precious promises, so that through them you may participate in the divine nature and escape the corruption in the world caused by evil desires" (2 Peter 1:3-4).

• "Resist the devil, and he will flee from you" (James 4:7).

• "No, in all these things we are more than conquerors through him who loved us" (Romans 8:37).

13

My Life Is Hopeless

LIE: *My life is hopeless.*

TRUTH: *My God is able to do exceedingly abundantly above all I can ask or think (Ephesians 3:20 NKJV).*

Horatio Spafford was born on October 20, 1828, in North Troy, New York. He was a successful lawyer in Chicago who was devoted to the Scriptures and his relationship to Jesus Christ. Sometime in 1871, just after Spafford had invested greatly in real estate, a devastating fire swept through Chicago, wiping out his holdings and his life savings. Just before the fire, he experienced the death of his only son.

Two years after the fire, Spafford planned a vacation to Europe for him and his family. He wanted to provide a respite for his wife and children and at the same time assist evangelist D.L. Moody with his campaigns in Great Britain. But at the last minute, just before their ship was to set sail, Spafford was called away on a business matter. He put his wife and four daughters on the S.S. Ville du Havre and kissed them good-bye with a promise to join them in a few days. But on November 22, the ship carrying Spafford's family was struck by an English vessel and quickly sank to the bottom of the Atlantic. In twelve short minutes, 226 lives met their watery grave; among them were all four of Spafford's daughters.

After the survivors were shuttled safely to shore in Wales, Spafford's wife cabled her husband with two simple words: "Saved alone."

Spafford left Chicago immediately to bring his grieving wife back home. As he passed near the place where his daughters took their last breaths, in the midst of his intense grief, he penned the words to one of my favorite hymns.

"It Is Well with My Soul"

When peace, like a river, attendeth my way,
When sorrows like sea billows roll;
Whatever my lot, Thou hast taught me to say,
It is well, it is well with my soul.

Refrain:
It is well (it is well),
With my soul (with my soul).
It is well, it is well with my soul.

Though Satan should buffet, though trials should come,
Let this blest assurance control,
That Christ hath regarded my helpless estate,
And hath shed His own blood for my soul.

My sin, oh, the bliss of this glorious thought!
My sin, not in part but the whole,
Is nailed to the cross, and I bear it no more,
Praise the Lord, praise the Lord, O my soul!

And Lord haste the day when my faith shall be sight,
The clouds be rolled back as a scroll;
The trump shall resound, and the Lord shall descend,
Even so, it is well with my soul.

The Storms of Life

God tells us we will have difficulties in this life. Jesus said, "In the world you have tribulation, but take courage; I have overcome the world" (John 17:33 NASB). How will we handle difficulties? What will we do? I can tell you what the enemy wants us to do. He wants us to give up...to quit. During difficult times he will tell us that the situation is hopeless: the disease is incurable, the loss irrecoverable, the decision irrevocable, the brokenness irreparable, the loss irretrievable, the sadness inconsolable, and the circumstances irreversible. And it is a lie.

All through the Bible, we see examples of God transforming seemingly hopeless situations into miraculous victories. He even gave the prophet Ezekiel a vision of a bunch of dried up bones being transformed into a mighty army (Ezekiel 37). Now if God can do that, he can certainly transform our broken lives.

When I was pregnant with my first child, I was extremely sick. I felt that I was on a rocking boat, tossed about by the swelling waves with no land in sight. However, I knew that in nine months the sickness would stop and I would hold a beautiful, much prayed-for baby in my arms. I kept saying to myself, *This light and momentary affliction is well worth the end result!*

I began to realize that most of life's most wonderful blessings begin with a painful situation. Many dreams are birthed through trials and struggles. Oh, that we had that attitude with each and every difficulty in life. And the good news is we can.

And It Came to Pass

One of my favorite expressions in the Bible is, "And it came to pass." Yes, I have taken that clause out of context, but it has proved to be true in my life. Life changes. Whether it is a poor grade in college, a desperate financial situation, or a slump in a marriage, the enemy will lie and tell us that it will always be that way—it will never change and we are without hope. However, the Bible tells us that there are seasons in life that we go through.

> There is a time for everything,
>> and a season for every activity under heaven
>> (Ecclesiastes 3:1).

Life is riddled with struggles that do indeed pass. But sometimes we simply give up too soon.

God reminded me of my propensity to give up too soon after

watching a NCAA tournament game with my family. It's called "March Madness," and in the Jaynes home, it's important.

It was Friday night, and my family and I were watching the University of North Carolina at Chapel Hill Tar Heels basketball team take on Southern California. All three of us had graduated from UNC, and we were pulling for the Tar Heels, but it wasn't looking too good for the home team. Halfway through the second half, we were down by 16 points.

"We're going to lose," we agreed.

"It's not worth staying up for," Steve said. "It's late. I'm tired. I don't want to watch them get creamed. They'll never come back from 16 points, and they look tired too."

So we turned off the television and said our goodnights. You can imagine our surprise Saturday morning when we opened the newspaper to read the headlines: "It's a Tar Heel Blitz!" They had come back to win the game 74-64…and we missed it.

I could almost hear God teasing me in the background, *See, you quit too soon…again.*

Sometimes when we're struggling and it looks like we're going to lose, we turn off the game and go to bed. But just because it looks like we're losing doesn't mean we are. The game's not over. God is still at work, and if we give up, we'll miss the thrill of victory. I don't know about you, but I don't want to hear about it secondhand or miss a single second of the miraculous win.

God Changes Our Circumstances

A certain widow in the Bible was in a desperate situation. She had run out of food, given up on life, and had no hope that her life would ever be any different. But just as she was about to make her final meal, God intervened.

Elijah, a prophet, had been living by the Kerith Ravine east of the Jordan. The people of Israel had been rebellious, so God sent a drought to get their attention. However, he provided for Elijah by sending him to live by a brook. He also sent ravens to bring him meat and bread in the evenings. Not a bad setup. Talk about fast food.

But even that was temporary. Sometime later, the brook dried up. Why would God provide water from the brook and then take that provision away? Because He had a grand plan to bless someone else. God sent Elijah to Zarephath where He had "commanded a widow" to supply Elijah with food. But when you read the story in the Bible, it appears that while God told Elijah, he forgot to tell the woman.

When Elijah arrived at this widow's house, she is gathering sticks to make her last meal. She looked in her pantry and discovered only enough flour and oil for one last loaf of bread. In her eyes, her dire situation was never going to change. This was it. This was the end.

What she didn't realize was that it was only the beginning. Let's join Elijah as he approaches this desperate woman.

> So he went to Zarephath. When he came to the town gate, a widow was there gathering sticks. He called to her and asked, "Would you bring me a little water in a jar so I may have a drink?" As she was going to get it, he called, "And bring me, please, a piece of bread."
>
> "As surely as the LORD your God lives," she replied, "I don't have any bread—only a handful of flour in a jar and a little oil in a jug. I am gathering a few sticks to take home and make a meal for myself and my son, that we may eat it—and die."
>
> Elijah said to her, "Don't be afraid. Go home and do as you have said. But first make a small cake of bread for me from what you have and bring it to me, and then make something for yourself and your son. For this is what the LORD, the God of Israel, says: 'The jar of flour will not be used up and the jug of oil will not run dry until the day the LORD gives rain on the land.'"
>
> She went away and did as Elijah had told her. So there was food every day for Elijah and for the woman and her family. For the jar of flour was not used up and the jug of oil did not run dry, in keeping with the word of the LORD spoken by Elijah (1 Kings 17:10-16).

Just when we think that life is hopeless, God intervenes. Don't let the enemy convince you that life cannot be any different than it is at the moment of your greatest need. It is simply not true. God is a God of miracles. While He never changes, He can certainly change our circumstances, as this letter I received attests:

> Dear Sharon,
>
> Twelve years ago, my home burned down and we lost everything. Ten months later, my husband died. He was only forty and I was thirty-seven. We had two teenage boys. I felt as though my life was over, but eight years later, I remarried. After this, life only got worse. My new husband and son were always at odds with each other. I remember sitting on the bathroom floor at my job sobbing and believing the only way out was to fall asleep and never wake up. I had the perfect plan and it almost worked.
>
> Our family had started attending church again. I had attended in the past, but had fallen away from my relationship with God. There was a woman at the church who listened to God and intervened in my suicide attempt. God literally reached down and saved my life. It was amazingly obvious that He put circumstances in place to keep me from following through with what I had planned.
>
> I surrendered my life to Jesus and began to pray that God would change me. That was three years ago, and I can honestly say my life is wonderful. My husband came to Christ and will be baptized in a few days. God brought me out of the pit, and I praise Him for all He has brought me through.

I read this letter and whispered a prayer of praise. I was so thankful that God had stopped Geri from taking her life. That is Satan's ultimate goal, you know. "The enemy comes only to steal and kill and destroy" (John 10:10). But suicide is a permanent solution to a temporary problem. *There is always hope.*

God Changes Our Perspective

I knew that nine months of morning sickness was going to conclude with the crashing cymbals of a baby's cry and a precious bundle in my arms. I knew there was an end in sight. But what if you don't know what the outcome will be? What if you can't see the light at the end of the tunnel? That's when we have to trust God.

Sometimes God does not change our difficult situations all at once. Most of the time it's a gradual unfolding of His divine plan. One author wrote this about healing: "Healing, I've learned, is hidden work. It's the touch of God on the tender, raw places of your soul. It's something you don't feel all at once, something you can't see. You don't mark that day on a calendar. You just look back over the weeks and months and realize you don't hurt the way you used to."[41]

One of the words used for God in the Old Testament indicates "one who comes alongside to rescue." Yes, He could rescue us from our circumstances, and many times He does. But He can also rescue us *in* our circumstances. Paul and Silas found themselves in quite a difficult situation. They were behind bars for teaching the good news of Jesus' resurrection and delivering a demon-possessed girl from an evil spirit. The girl could no longer tell fortunes, and her employer was furious about her deliverance and his loss of income. Paul and Silas were arrested, flogged, and locked in the inner chambers with their feet in stocks.

So what did they do as they sat bloodied, condemned, and chained? They began singing and praying. Yes, singing! Suddenly, as the other prisoners were listening to the music, God made a little of His own. A violent earthquake shook the foundations of the prison and the doors flew open. Everybody's chains fell off (see Acts 16).

When we begin to praise God in our circumstances, others watching and listening are blessed as well. Who knows, your trust in God may be the vehicle through which others are freed from their personal chains.

God says, "Was my arm too short to ransom you? Do I lack the strength to rescue you?" (Isaiah 50:2). Your difficult circumstances may feel too deep to climb out of, too high to reach up to, or too wide to stretch your arms around. But the arm of God is never too short to reach down and pull you out, reach up and draw you near, or reach around you and hold you close.

One of my favorite movies is *It's a Wonderful Life* about a man named George Bailey. You probably know the story. George lived in a small town, and his father ran the local building and loan. George vowed he would get out of that horse-and-buggy town and see the world. But life didn't turn out as George had hoped.

After his father died of a stroke, George's dreams of seeing the world and going to college were dashed. Several years later he had a mortgage, a wife, and three adorable kids. One Christmas Eve, his absent-minded Uncle Billy, who worked at the bank with him, misplaced a sizable amount of cash. With this sudden shortfall, George faced bankruptcy and possible jail time. He saw no way out of this desperate situation. "I wish I had never been born," he cried.

George was just about to take his own life when an angel named Clarence appeared. Throughout the rest of the movie, Clarence takes George on a stroll through his life to show him just what would have happened if he had never been born. His brother, Harry, would have drowned as a child. Mary, George's wife, would have become an old maid. The local druggist would have been in prison for giving the wrong medication to a patient. Other tragedies were averted because of George's life.

By the end of the movie, George realizes he has had an exceptional life, and he rushes home with a new perspective. His circumstances hadn't changed, but his perspective changed everything.

Sometimes God changes our circumstances and sometimes He changes how we view them. Life is never hopeless because we serve an amazing God who is all about miraculous change and victory.

It Is Well with My Soul

I wish I could tell you that each time life throws me a curveball, I strike up the chorus of "It is well with my soul." I wish I could tell you that when my baby died, I hummed that familiar tune. Or that when the pregnancy test read negative for the thirty-sixth time, I sang those words. I wish I could tell you that the day my father looked me in the eyes and couldn't remember my name because of Alzheimer's disease, I whistled this beloved hymn. But that wasn't the case. I grieved. I mourned. I cried in despair.

But God (don't you love all the "but God's" in the Bible) *has taught me to say,* It is well with my soul. How? By replacing the lies with the truth. Oh, the situations did not change. My baby was still on the other side, I never got pregnant again, and my father was not healed from Alzheimer's. The circumstances did not change, but my perspective did.

I began to see that my baby was with Jesus. I began to see that God had a greater plan for my life that involved spiritual children all around the world. I began to see that my heavenly father would never forget my name.

It is well with my soul.

• • • **RECOGNIZE THE LIE:** My life is hopeless.

• • • **REJECT THE LIE:** That is not true.

• • • **REPLACE THE LIE WITH TRUTH:**

- "Find rest, O my soul, in God alone; my hope comes from him. He alone is my rock and my salvation; he is my fortress, I will not be shaken" (Psalm 62:5-6).

- "But as for me, I will always have hope; I will praise you more and more" (Psalm 71:14).

- "For our light and momentary troubles are achieving for us an eternal glory that far outweighs them all. So we fix our eyes not on what is seen, but on what is unseen. For what is seen is temporary, but what is unseen is eternal" (2 Corinthians 4:17).

14

God Doesn't Love Me

LIE: *God doesn't love me.*

TRUTH: *God loves me totally, completely, and immeasurably (Ephesians 3:17-19).*

When I was a little girl, my father spent most of his waking hours working at his building supply company, observing construction sites, or socializing with his colleagues and associates. Even though his place of business was only a few blocks from our home, his heart was miles away in a place I could not find. My father didn't drink alcohol every day, but when he did, it consumed him. Dad was filled with a rage that always seemed to be hiding just beneath the surface of his tough skin. But when he drank, that rage spewed out like hot lava onto those around him.

As a child, many nights I crawled into bed, pulled the covers tightly under my chin or over my head, and prayed that I would hurry and fall asleep to shut out the noise of my parents fighting. Occasionally I'd tiptoe over to my pink ballerina jewelry box, wind up the music key in the back, and try to focus on the tinkling sound that came as the ballerina twirled with hands overhead.

I was afraid of my father. Even when he was sober, I kept my distance.

At the same time, I observed how other daddies cherished their little girls. I saw them cuddle them in their laps, hold their hands while walking in the park, or kiss their cheeks as they dropped them off in the mornings at school. Deep in my heart, a dream was birthed. I dreamed that one day I would have a daddy who loved me—not because I was pretty or made good grades or could play the piano well, but just because I was his.

A Dream Come True

In the Old Testament, God has many names, but in the New Testament, Jesus emphasizes God's role as our *Father*. It is the name that Jesus referred to more than any other and the name that He invites us to use to address the Creator of the universe. Just stop and think about that for a moment. The God of all creation, who always has been and always will be, who is all-knowing, all-powerful, and present everywhere at once—that same God invites you to call Him *Daddy!* He said, "I will be a Father to you, and you will be my sons and daughters" (2 Corinthians 6:18).

For many, the idea of God being their father may not be a pleasant one. We have a tendency to project our perception of fatherhood, based on our experience with our earthly fathers, onto our idea of the fatherhood of God. Some never knew their earthly fathers, some had abusive fathers, some were deserted by their fathers, some had loving endearing fathers, and some lost their fathers due to sickness or catastrophe. Even the best earthly fathers have feet of clay and will disappoint their children.

No matter what your past experience has been with your earthly father, the truth is your heavenly Father is the perfect parent who loves you, cares for your every need, is interested in all you do, skillfully guides you, wisely trains you, never deserts you, generously supplies for your needs, is always available to you, and cherishes you as His precious child. He loves you with an everlasting love. He is especially fond of *you*.

God's Unconditional Love

Unfortunately, we live in a world of performance-based acceptance. We grow up believing, "If I make good grades, my parents will love me. If I keep my room clean, my mom will approve of me. If I make the team, my friends will admire me. If I am pretty, the boys will like me. If I cook great meals, keep the house clean, and perform well in bed, my husband will love me. If I meet my deadlines, make no mistakes, and get to work on time, my boss will reward me. If I call my mother three times a week, visit her once a week, and spend every Christmas and Thanksgiving at her house, then she will approve of me. If I..."

From the time we exit the safety of a mother's womb, we enter a world of performance-based acceptance. It's what we've grown to expect. But friend, God does not love us on the merit of our behavior. He loves us just because we're His.

I love these words Paul wrote to the Ephesians:

> For he chose us in him before the creation of the world to be holy and blameless in his sight. In love he predestined us to be adopted as his sons through Jesus Christ, in *accordance with his pleasure* and will—to the praise of his glorious grace, which he has freely given us in the One he loves...And he made known to us the mystery of his will *according to his good pleasure,* which he purposed in Christ, to be put into effect when the times will have reached their fulfillment—to bring all things in heaven and on earth together under one head, even Christ (Ephesians 1:4-6, 9-10, emphasis added).

Why does God love us so much? Because He wants to. Because of His good pleasure.

In the Old Testament, the Israelites were commanded to follow all manner of rules and regulations. They thought that if they followed the law without fail, they would be acceptable to God. But there was no way the people could remember all those rules and regulations, much less obey them.

I believe one reason God gave the Old Covenant was to show that we are helpless to earn our way to heaven on our own. No one could ever perform perfectly. It is simply not in our nature or ability to do so. "All our righteous acts are like filthy rags," the prophet Isaiah said (Isaiah 64:6).

So God sent His Son, Jesus Christ, who gave His perfect sinless life as a sacrifice for our mistakes and sins. Jesus' last words were, "It is finished." The debt was paid in full, and we never have to perform for our acceptance again. He did what we are unable to do—once and for all. Why did God do such a thing? Why did He give His only Son so that we could be forgiven, cleansed, and free from our sins? Because He loves me so much. Because He loves you so much (John 3:16).

Here's an interesting twist though. God doesn't love us because we perform well, but if we love Him we will. Jesus said if we love him we will obey him (John 14:15,23). A desire to please God will flow from a heart that loves Him.

But God loves us regardless of our actions. That is difficult for our human minds to grasp because we're not naturally wired that way. His ways are so much higher than our ways, and His love is unconditional, unchanging, unfathomable, immeasurable.

God's Infinitely Wise Ways

"Mommy, Mommy," Steven cried. "Don't let them hurt me!"

My son was two years old when he contracted a severe case of the flu. He slumped listlessly in my lap like an old worn rag doll. When I carried him into the medical clinic, the doctor quickly surmised that Steven was dehydrated and needed to be admitted into the hospital immediately.

My heart broke as the nurses strapped my little boy onto a table and began placing IVs in his tiny arms. "Mommy," he cried, "make them stop! They're hurting me."

"No, honey," I tried to assure him. "They're going to make you all better."

Steven cried. I cried. The nurses cried.

I could only imagine what was going through Steven's little mind: *Why are these people hurting me? Why doesn't Mommy make them stop?*

She must not love me. She's not protecting me. If she loved me she wouldn't let them do this. She must not care about me.

Standing in the corner watching my little boy cry, I wondered if how I was feeling is how God feels when I'm going through painful situations that are for my good. I cry, *God, why are You letting this happen? Don't You love me? Don't You care about what's happening to me? Why don't You make them stop?*

Then God seemed to reply, *Sometimes you are like this little lamb. You don't understand the purpose for the pain and often think I have deserted you. But I will never leave you. You think that I don't love you, but I love you to the height of heaven and the depth of the sea. You think that I don't care about what's happening to you, but I am orchestrating your days and care about every hair on your head. My ways are higher than your ways and My thoughts higher than your thoughts. Yes, I do care about you and what is happening to you. I am bringing you to spiritual health and wholeness.*

Even when I don't understand, when I can't see His plan, I know that all His ways are loving and kind. He knows what's best for me, and He is always good.

> "So do not fear, for I am with you;
>   do not be dismayed, for I am your God.
> I will strengthen you and help you;
>   I will uphold you with my righteous right hand"
>   (Isaiah 41:10).

God's Infinite Ways Are Good

I hopped up on the counter at the soda fountain and placed my five-year-old feet on the spinning stool in front of me. Dad sipped on a Coke and talked to the lady behind the counter with the red-and-white-striped apron tied around her waist.

"This is my little girl," Daddy said with a smile. "She's a little monkey."

"Why Allan, she's just as cute as she can be."

I thought for a moment I was.

. . . . .

I stood in the front yard of a ranch-style house waiting for the screaming to stop before I went back inside. Dad was drunk again, and Mom was screaming at the top of her lungs. Why couldn't he see how afraid I was? Why did he drink? Why did Mom yell? Why did they hit each other? After twelve years of these volcanic outbursts, you'd think I'd be used to it. But it always came as a surprise.

The next day came with many promises. "I'll never do it again," Dad said. "I am so sorry, Sharon. I'll never come home like that again."

But there was always a next time.

. . . . .

I stretched on tiptoes among the crowd of seniors on the stage. I had just been admitted into the National Honor Society along with several of my friends. Cameras snapped, proud parents cheered, and boys and girls waved at admiring parents. But my parents were not among the beaming parents in the auditorium that day. Later my dad explained: "The school called the night before and told me about the induction ceremony, but I fell asleep on the couch and forgot all about it. I'm sorry, Sharon. It won't happen again."

But it did.

. . . . .

Once we grasp the truth of God's amazing love, we come to the next question: Can I trust Him? Can I trust God with my hopes and fears, days and years? When you understand the depth of His love, the answer is always yes. Perfect love drives away all fear (1 John 4:18).

When I fully grasped the idea that God loved me, I hung onto that truth like a girl overboard gasping for air. I could relate to the rejected Jesus and easily accepted the indescribable gift He gave. I marveled at

God's love. I truly did. But when it came time to trust God with my hopes and dreams, that was a different story. When conflicts arose, I became that teenage girl looking in the crowd for a daddy who wasn't there. Could I trust this heavenly Father? I wasn't so sure.

But one day, God spoke to my heart in a poignant way. *Take your father's face off of Me,* He seemed to say. *I am not like your earthly father. I am your heavenly Father.*

I am always good.
I always tell the truth.
I want what is best for you.
You can trust Me.

God Is Always Good

It is easy to trust God when life is good. But when a child rebels, the bank account dwindles, or the biopsy comes back malignant, we wonder, *Is God really good?* We know in our heads that God is good, but the heart struggles to believe. The enemy continues to peddle the lie that God is not good—He is holding out on us. That's what He told Eve. *God is holding out on you. You can't trust Him. You will not die.*

Life is filled with disappointment. And it's during those times of disappointment when the enemy sows seeds of distrust with thoughts of mistrust.

When I was struggling all those years with infertility, the enemy continually taunted me with, *God doesn't love you. If He loved you He would give you what you want. He would give you a child. You can't trust Him with your heart. You can't trust Him with your dreams.*

When we lost our second child in a miscarriage, the enemy pestered me with, *How could God let this happen? How could He break your heart like this? How could a loving God allow such pain?*

Have you ever felt that way? I think, for most of us, the enemy has whispered those lies into our minds. But the truth is, if God says *no* in one area of our lives, it's because He has a greater *yes* in store.

Can't you imagine how the disciples felt as the stone was rolled in front of Jesus' tomb? *How could this happen? Where is God?* But three days later, when Jesus rose from the grave and appeared to them in all His glory, they knew the answer. God had a greater plan.

God is good...all the time. No matter what twists and turns happen in our lives, God is good. We live in a fallen world where bad things happen. People get sick and die. Accidents take lives. Hurricanes, tsunamis, and earthquakes rip lands apart. Evil people kill and destroy. Death and disappointment are part of life.

But God is still good...all the time. As the psalmist wrote, "You are good, and what you do is good" (Psalm 119:68).

God Always Tells the Truth

One of the many reasons we can trust God is He always tells the truth. He *is* truth.

David was a man in deep distress. For years he had been chased by King Saul, who was determined to kill him. His eyes were weak with sorrow and his soul and body worn with grief.

> My life is consumed by anguish
>   and my years by groaning;
> my strength fails because of my affliction,
>   and my bones grow weak.
> Because of all my enemies,
>   I am the utter contempt of my neighbors;
> I am a dread to my friends—
>   those who see me on the street flee from me.
> I am forgotten by them as though I were dead;
>   I have become like broken pottery
>   (Psalm 31:10-12).

David was in dire straits, and even though the prophet Samuel had anointed him as the next king of Israel, he was living like a criminal on the run.

I might have thought, *King? Did you say king? This doesn't look like a king's life to me.*

But rather than turn his back on God, he turned his face toward Him.

> But I trust in you, O LORD;
> I say, "You are my God"
> (Psalm 31:14).

What gave him the impetus to trust God in the face of incredible struggles? He already had made a decision in his heart that God always tells the truth—and truth gives birth to trust. King David faced very difficult times, and yet he prayed,

> Into your hands I commit my spirit;
> redeem me, O LORD, the *God of truth*
> (Psalm 31:5, emphasis added).

What makes it difficult to trust others? The feeling that they are not looking out for our best interests or they do not always tell the truth. But God is always looking out for our best interests and He always tells the truth. "Let God be true, and every man a liar" (Romans 3:4). "God is not a man, that he should lie" (Numbers 23:19). "It is impossible for God to lie" (Hebrews 6:18).

No matter what anyone else says, God always tells the truth.

God Wants What Is Best for You

I stood on the edge of the Grand Canyon, amazed at the magnitude of the majestic beauty. I could scarcely take it in. Even a wide-angle camera lens didn't begin to capture the expanse. And yet, when I had flown over it the day before, I had seen it from beginning to end in a single majestic sweep.

Once again I was reminded about God's perspective of my life. I have only a few pieces of the puzzle, but God holds the box top. I have no idea what the grand portrait of my life is going to look like in the end, but God holds the brush and knows exactly what strokes belong where.

The enemy tells us that *we* know what's best for our lives, and if we're honest, we think we know what's best for others as well. But the truth is, we have no idea. Oh sure, we do know the ultimate best, which is summed up in two words—Follow Jesus. Jesus said, "I am the way and the truth and the life." When we walk with Him, He will show us the way, one step at a time, without worry.

Worry is the opposite of trust. One definition of *worry* is "to seize by the throat with teeth and shake or mangle as one animal does another, or to harass by repeated biting or snapping."[42]

That's exactly what Satan does with his prey. He harasses us with "what ifs" until our minds are confused.

All worry is wrapped in the lie that God is not to be trusted. If we truly believe the truth that God loves us, God is good, God always tells us the truth, and God wants what is best for us, then we will not worry. The future is in God's hands, and His plans are good.

"Cast all your anxiety on him," Peter wrote, "because he cares for you" (1 Peter 5:7). Another translation says it this way: "Let him have all your worries and cares, for he is always thinking about you and watching everything that concerns you" (TLB).

Like a passenger who keeps grabbing the steering wheel, we tend to grab for control in our lives. We believe the lie that we know what's best and so try to steer things the direction we think they should go. When that happens, we run off the road, take wrong turns, and often run out of gas.

I read a bumper sticker that said, "God is my co-pilot." If that's the case in your life, then you need to switch seats.

> "No eye has seen,
>   no ear has heard,
>   no mind has conceived
>   what God has prepared for those who love him"
>   (1 Corinthians 2:9).

God loves you. God is good. God always tells the truth. God wants what's best for you. And you can trust Him. That's the truth.

• • • **RECOGNIZE THE LIE:** God doesn't love me.

• • • **REJECT THE LIE:** That is not true.

• • • **REPLACE THE LIE WITH TRUTH:**

- "I trust in God's unfailing love forever and ever" (Psalm 52:8).

- "For I am convinced that neither death nor life, neither angels nor demons, neither the present nor the future, nor any powers, neither height nor depth, nor anything else in all creation, will be able to separate us from the love of God that is in Christ Jesus our Lord" (Romans 8:38-39).

- "But because of his great love for us, God, who is rich in mercy, made us alive with Christ even when we were dead in transgressions and sins—it is by grace you have been saved" (Ephesians 2:4-5).

- "This is love: not that we loved God, but that he loved us and sent his Son as an atoning sacrifice for our sins" (1 John 4:10).

- "God is love" (1 John 4:16).

15

God Is Punishing Me

LIE: *God is punishing me.*

TRUTH: *God is purifying me as gold (1 Peter 1:6-7).*

My son, Steven, and I sat on the floor in his room playing rummy. We had just a few minutes before rushing off to register for his summer swim class and wanted to get in one more round of play. This summer was proving to be the best ever. Our golden retriever, Ginger, had just delivered seven adorable puppies, Steven was enjoying his sixth summer of life, and after four years of doctor visits, infertility treatments, and negative pregnancy tests, God had surprised us with a precious gift. The stick turned blue.

But as Steven and I sat on the floor that bright summer day, I felt a warm sticky sensation run down my leg, and the sun began to set on my hopes and dreams. A trip to the bathroom confirmed my greatest fear. Later that afternoon, the doctor confirmed, "There is no heartbeat."

What began as a summer full of life and joy quickly turned into a season of great loss and sadness. I mourned for that child I had prayed for and felt the ache of empty arms. Someone once said, "I never knew I could miss someone I had never met." But oh, how I missed her. We never knew for sure, but in my heart I felt that the baby had been a little girl.

After the loss, in the quiet of night, the enemy hissed, *God doesn't love you. If He loved you He wouldn't have let this happen. This is your*

fault, you know. You didn't have enough faith. He's punishing you.
You're not good enough to have another child. Bad things happen to bad
people.

You know what? I began to believe him. I bought the lie. "God,
are You punishing me?" I cried. "What have I done to deserve this?
Don't You care about me?"

I was so weak and weary, I didn't have the strength to fight the
enemy. That's when my friends locked arms and believed God for
me. They prayed and loved me back to my senses. That's what friends
are for.

Rather than crying out "Why me?" I began earnestly praying,
"What now." "What do you want me to do now, Lord?"

Many questions rumbled around in my mind, but the thought
that God was punishing me remained the loudest. It is a common
question rooted in the lie that God is not a loving God. And that has
the smell of smoke all over it.

I believe when we go through a trial that wounds us deeply, God
can use it to teach us valuable lessons. Some of these lessons are a
deeper understanding of who He is, of who we are, and of what we
truly believe. Our faith grows in the petri dish of struggles in the
laboratory of life.

Why Do Bad Things Happen?

There is no easy answer to the question of why tragedy strikes.
Is it God's discipline, the devil's deception, or the result of living in
a degenerate fallen world? Each one of these is a viable option, but
we mustn't be too quick to assume it's because of something we've
done.

Yes, God does discipline us. The Bible says, "Know then in your
heart that as a man disciplines his son, so the LORD your God disciplines you" (Deuteronomy 8:5). And:

> My son, do not despise the LORD's discipline
>   and do not resent his rebuke,

because the LORD disciplines those he loves,
    as a father the son he delights in
        (Proverbs 3:11-12).

However, every time we read about God disciplining someone in the Bible, that person knew exactly Who was doing the punishing and why He was doing it.

God disciplined Miriam for gossiping about her brother Moses (Numbers 12). God disciplined Saul for acting like a self-appointed priest (1 Samuel 13). God struck down Ananias and Sapphira when they lied about how much money they put in the offering plate (Acts 5). In each case, there was not a hint of repentance from the offenders and no question as to why they were being punished.

We also read the stories of Job and Peter that show that sometimes difficulties are due to spiritual attack. God granted Satan permission to test both of these men. Both came out of the battle stronger, holier, and more powerful than ever. So sometimes difficult situations are due to an all-out attack from the enemy.

The Bible tells us that God quickly forgives when we repent and ask. He does not keep a record of wrongs and punish us for past sins. He throws our sins into the deepest of seas and doesn't go back to fish them out. He simply does not work that way.

Sometimes we have to live with the consequences of our sin and that can feel like punishment. But we must always remember that consequences are a result of our choices. Sexually transmitted diseases and unplanned pregnancies can be the consequences of sexual promiscuity. Broken relationships are a consequence of lying.

If you jump out of a second story building and break your leg, you would not say God is punishing you by breaking your leg. You broke your leg. It is a consequence of a bad choice.

There is no pat answer as to why bad things happen. Ultimately, God is in control, and His ways are higher than our ways (Isaiah 55:8-9). In *When God Doesn't Make Sense,* Dr. James Dobson says, "Trying to analyze [God's] omnipotence is like an amoeba attempting to comprehend the behavior of man."[43] It's simply not possible.

Face to Face with the Father

Shannon is a friend of mine who also questioned whether God was punishing her through infertility. She described her doctor's words as "a constant, haunting hum in her head, like a song you can't shake—a song with the power to drive you insane. His voice was inescapable. 'You're infertile,' I heard before breakfast, and again in the late afternoon when the light dipped and faded, and yet again in the black, middle-of-the-night hours when I ached for sleep but couldn't make my eyes close."[44]

Through many years of doctor visits, failed adoptions, and negative pregnancy tests, Shannon wondered if she were being punished by God. When she was nineteen, Shannon walked through the doors of an abortion clinic to terminate the life of her unborn child. However, a test before the procedure proved that she was not pregnant. But the guilt from what she had intended to do followed her like a dark cloud. *Could it be that God is punishing me?* she wondered through the years of infertility. *Perhaps I'm not good enough for Him to bless me.* But it took hearing the lie from a coworker to slap her with the truth.

> I wanted to be a powerful teacher. I wanted to make God proud. So in addition to my regular Bible reading and my scheduled prayers, I started reading Romans every week…I comforted myself with the hope that my studious diligence would pay off in the only way that mattered.
>
> Somewhere deep down, I must have believed that God would notice how smart as a whip I was and grade me accordingly. He'd remove the F I received the day I walked into that abortion clinic with its rainbow sign and its filthy floor, and he'd replace it with an A+. When he did that—when he nodded his approval and expunged my record—he'd let me know by sending the only message that could possibly convince me: He'd let me conceive.
>
> About a year after I began my Romans-fest, I began a job as a hostess in the apartment clubhouse where we lived. I'd take my

Bible and notebook and sit in the center of the lounge where I could keep an eye on the pool and greet the residents who popped in.

I had my tally sheet and much-marked book of Romans lying open one evening when a maintenance worker walked in to get a cup of coffee. He saw my Bible and asked what I was reading.

"Romans," I said.

He nodded. "Good book."

We talked about where we each fellowshipped for a moment, and then he made an odd pronouncement. "Yea, I learned my lesson this week."

"How's that?"

"Last Sunday I forgot to tithe. And guess what happened Monday?"

I couldn't guess.

"I got a flat tire."

I sat waiting for the punch line, unable to track with his thinking.

"Don't you get it? The flat tire was a message: 'If you want me to bless you, you've got to keep up your end of the deal.' God will not be mocked. He was warning me."

"No, he wasn't." The words galloped out of my mouth before I could fling a rope around them.

"He sure was."

Now we were into it. I tossed all restraint aside. "You think God only blesses you when you're good?"

"Sure do. If you follow the rules, give him what belongs to him, and don't mess up, good things will happen to you. If you don't do all that, bad things follow."

"How can you even *think* that? Who taught you that garbage?"

"You calling the Word of God garbage? 'Will a man rob God… Bring the whole tithe into the storehouse…Test me in this,' says the LORD Almighty, 'and see if I will not throw open the flood-gates of heaven and pour out so much blessing that you will not have room enough for it' " (Malachi 3:8,10).

"Yes…but…but to talk about God as if he's vindictive and petty and…and…like us."

"If you want to be blessed, you've got to hold up your end of the bargain." He picked up his cup, gave me a firm and dismissive nod, and marched out of the clubhouse.

I stared after him. How could a person think that way? How could you love or serve a God that petty? I couldn't figure it out. I certainly didn't know his God…

Oh, don't you?

The thought echoed in the stunned silence of my mind. For a long, horrible moment I sat and let the ramifications of that question pelt and taunt me.

But then I stood, plugged in the vacuum cleaner, and drowned out the echo.

I didn't read a word of my Bible the next day. I had a good excuse—friends from California had called earlier in the week to visit. After catching up on our lives, we said our goodnights. I didn't sleep well. Untended business tugged at me. So at 5:00 a.m., with only a few hours' sleep behind me, I took my Bible and crept into the bathroom—the only room where I could read and not disturb anyone else.

I opened my Bible to a familiar spot and sat on the floor with my back against the wall—both literally and figuratively. God had me cornered. That blasted maintenance worker had pulled all my sleepy thoughts from my mind, laid them out on the table, and slapped them awake—and now I was going to have to claim them for my own.

I *did* think of God that way. I thought I could make him owe me.

It's more than that, I heard.

So he wanted to get it all out. He wanted to fillet me, right there, and remove every cancerous thought growing on my mind.

"It's more than what?"

You think you can earn blessings—and you think you have to erase your mistakes to make me love you.

I looked at the open Bible in my lap and, suddenly, all the red marked verses began to leap off the page at me: "justified by faith...whose sins have been covered...reconciled to God...free gift...made righteous..." (Romans 3:28; 4:7; 5:10,15,19 NASB).

Then my eyes flew back a few verses to the one that finally broke through: "For while we were still helpless, at the right time Christ died for the ungodly" (Romans 5:6 NASB).

The words I'd read every week for a year breathed and sat up and stretched their arms wide, and I fell into them. And God whispered a revelation. *When you were head over heels in love with your sin, that's when I chose you. When you were as far from me as you could possibly be, that's when I said, "She's mine."*

He had planned it all. God drove me to that bathroom and set me on that floor, and when I looked around I realized where I was, and remembered that long-ago bathroom when I sat in that same position and begged him to empty my womb, he was right there to whisper what I most needed to hear:

I was there—and I wept with you.

I wasn't being punished. I wasn't paying for a mistake. God wasn't angry with me.

I pulled my Bible up tight against my chest, lifted my face toward his, and sobbed. He offered, and I let him take from me all the hatred I'd held for myself, all the fear I'd held toward him, and every doubt I'd held about my past and how it affected my future.

In the quiet of that room I heard a promise:

I will be your very great reward.[45]

The Promise of Trouble

God was not punishing Shannon. She knew that now. This was simply His plan for her.

When we go through struggles, the enemy will try to convince us that we are being punished for some sin in our lives. Yes, God does discipline His children. Yes, we do face the consequences of choosing sin in our lives. However, we cannot throw a blanket of condemnation over all our trials and struggles. Abraham, Isaac, Jacob, Joseph, Moses, Joshua, David, the prophets, the disciples, Paul, and even Jesus experienced more trouble in their lives than you and I could even imagine. And yet, these were God's chosen instruments to bring His kingdom message. Do you think Satan whispered these same lies to these men? There's no doubt in my mind that he did.

Jesus said, "In this world *you will have* trouble. But take heart! I have overcome the world" (John 16:33).

James wrote, "Consider it pure joy, my brothers, *whenever* you face trials of many kinds, because you know that the testing of your faith develops perseverance" (James 1:2).

Peter wrote, "In this you greatly rejoice, though now for a little while you may have had to suffer grief in all kinds of trials. These have come *so that* your faith—of greater worth than gold, which perishes even though refined by fire—may be proved genuine and may result in praise, glory and honor when Jesus Christ is revealed" (1 Peter 1:6-7).

Trouble. Trials. Suffering. They are all a part of living in a fallen world. Satan tries to tell us that suffering is our fault. "You deserve it," he taunts. "God's punishing you," he hisses. "You're no good."

Lies. All lies.

Oh sure, Job did question God in the end. And God answered Job in such a mighty way. It's worth going back and reading. But the outcome of Job's collective calamity was a greater knowledge of who God is and what God does. At the conclusion of Job's suffering he said,

> "My ears had heard of you
> but now my eyes have seen you"
> (Job 42:5).

Isn't that what we all want? To experience God in such a real way that we can sense His hand on the cool of our brow, to feel His breath on the nape of our neck, to warm in His embrace around our feeble shoulders? Is there any more priceless treasure to be excavated from the trials of life than discovering more of God?

That is not punishment, my friend. That is a blessing.

••• **RECOGNIZE THE LIE:** God is punishing me.

••• **REJECT THE LIE:** That is not true.

••• **REPLACE THE LIE WITH TRUTH:**

- "As he went along, he saw a man blind from birth. His disciples asked him, 'Rabbi, who sinned, this man or his parents, that he was born blind?' 'Neither this man nor his parents sinned,' said Jesus, 'but this happened so that the work of God might be displayed in his life'" (John 9:1-3).

- "Consider it pure joy, my brothers, whenever you face trials of many kinds, because you know that the testing of your faith develops perseverance. Perseverance must finish its work so that you may be mature and complete, not lacking anything" (James 1:2-4).

- "Dear friends, do not be surprised at the painful trial you are suffering, as though something strange were happening to you. But rejoice that you participate in the sufferings of Christ, so that you may be overjoyed when his glory is revealed" (1 Peter 4:12-13).

16

I'm Not Good Enough to Be a Christian

LIE: *I'm not good enough to be a Christian.*

TRUTH: *"For it is by grace you have been saved, through faith—and this not from yourselves, it is the gift of God—not by works, so that no one can boast" (Ephesians 2:8-9).*

I walked through the receiving line during the memorial service for a godly man who had passed away a few days before. As the man in front of me embraced the wounded widow, he whispered, "Oh, but you will see him again." My heart broke as I heard her reply, "I hope so. I don't know if I've been good enough."

This was no place for me to reprimand or scold, but my heart was torn in two.

This 86-year-old woman had been in church all her life. She read her Bible often, pondered devotions daily, and attended church regularly. And yet, she believed a lie. Somehow she believed that she had to earn her way to heaven…that she had to be "good enough to get in."

Oh, dear friend, we will never be good enough to earn our way to heaven. We will never be good enough to "get in." If we could, Jesus never would have had to give His life in our stead. It is a free gift.

So many are trying to earn what they already have. And it is the lie of performance-based acceptance that keeps women bound.

Perhaps you've found yourself believing the lie that you have to earn your way to heaven, or that you could somehow lose your salvation if you did not perform properly. Let's expose that lie and learn to walk in God's incredible gift of grace.

Or perhaps you have the helmet of salvation fixed securely in place, and it has never left your pretty little head. If that's the case, just sit back and thank God for it. Then rejoice with your sisters who are about to pluck the bow from God's most precious gift and join the party.

What Does It Mean to Be Saved?

The word *saved* has been tossed about so much in the church that it has lost its wonder and mystery. What does it mean to be saved?

Salvation means "deliverance" or "rescue." So what are we delivered or rescued from? Through Jesus Christ we are rescued from lostness (Luke 19:10), the wrath of God (Romans 5:9), the penalty of sin (Romans 6:23), the realm of darkness (Colossians 1:13), eternal separation from God, and eternal punishment in hell (Revelation 20:6). We *are saved* from the penalty of sin the moment we believe. We *are being saved* from the power of sin as we continue more and more to be conformed to the image of Christ. And we *will be saved* from the presence of sin when we leave this earthly body to spend eternity with God.

Saving faith involves our entire being: mind, will, and emotions. With the mind we understand the truth of the gospel, with the will we choose to submit to God and make Jesus Lord of our lives, and with the emotions we express sorrow over our sin and joy over God's mercy and grace. Salvation is more than a "get out of jail free" card. It is more than a ticket into heaven. Eternal life begins the moment we believe, and God's desire is for us to experience the abundant life here on earth (John 10:10). It is passing from spiritual death to spiritual life in the twinkling of God's eye. We are not saved by how we behave but by how we believe.

What Does It Mean to Be Lost?

It was our first trip to Disney World, and my video camera was poised to capture those precious memories. But the video didn't start out as I had planned. As it begins, we're in a welcoming center where children are climbing on various objects, crawling through tunnels, and swinging from monkey bars. Then we see my husband, Steve, running toward the camera, his face growing larger and larger until it fills the frame.

"Where's Steven?" he cries. "I can't find him anywhere!"

Then the screen goes blank.

What a way to start our vacation. Steven had wandered away, climbed into one of those tunnels, and had yet to emerge. Of course we panicked. Who wants to lose their kid at Disney World? Of course we found him. He had no idea he was even lost.

Ah, did that last sentence give you pause?

Even as I wrote it, God quickly reminded me that I was once in the same situation. I had no idea I was lost, but my Heavenly Father found me.

Lost. What does it mean to be lost? How did we get into this situation of such lostness, darkness, and emptiness? It all began in the Garden of Eden when man chose to disobey God and sever their relationship. The Bible tells us that from the moment Eve sank her teeth into the forbidden fruit, her body lived, but her spirit died. Every person since that time has been born with a live body and soul but a dead spirit—separated from God. Rejected. But God did not leave us that way. As soon as Adam and Eve disobeyed God, the shadow of the cross appeared on the horizon, and God began to unfold His magnificent redemptive plan.

After Adam and Eve disobeyed, they hid from God. When He came looking for them in the cool of the evening, He asked the first question recorded in the Bible: *Where are you?* That question runs like a scarlet thread from Genesis through Revelation.

Where are you? No matter what you've done, no matter how far you've strayed from His perfect plan for your life, He is always in pursuit of you. All you have to do is come out from hiding and say, *Here I am, Lord.*

From Genesis through Revelation, we see that plan unfurl right before our eyes. The Book of Romans outlines the steps of salvation beautifully. Let's take a walk down the Roman Road to discover how to move from rejected to accepted…how to receive the gift of eternal life tomorrow and abundant life today.

The Problem

"For all have sinned and fall short of the glory of God" (Romans 3:23).

Not one person has ever been good enough go to heaven on his own merits except Jesus Christ. No one can work his way to heaven. This is perhaps one of the greatest differences between Christianity and other world religions. Buddhism, Hinduism, and Islam all teach that we have to earn our way to God. Guess what. We can't.

Imagine you are standing on the east coast of the United States, peering out over the Atlantic Ocean. On the opposite shore, God is sitting on His throne. All you have to do is put on your goggles and flippers and swim to the other side. Would you make it? No. Likewise, there is no way that you or I could ever work our way into heaven. God requires sinless perfection in order to enter into His presence, and as the writer of Romans reminds us, we've all failed.

The Penalty

"For the wages of sin is death, but the gift of God is eternal life in Christ Jesus our Lord" (Romans 6:23).

From the very beginning, God warned Adam and Eve that if they disobeyed Him and ate the forbidden fruit, the penalty would be death. And while their bodies did not die the moment they sinned, the process was set in motion, and their spirits died totally and completely.

Through one act of disobedience, the dike was opened and creation was flooded with sin. However, just as one act of disobedience ushered sin into the world, one act of obedience delivered grace. Jesus Christ's sacrifice made eternal life available to all who believe. Notice that Paul refers to eternal life as a *gift*. Salvation is not something we earn.

It is not a paycheck at the end of a long life. It is a gift to be received, unwrapped, and enjoyed forever.

In his letter to the Ephesians Paul wrote, "But because of his great love for us, God, who is rich in mercy, made us alive with Christ even when we were dead in transgressions...For it is by *grace* you have been saved, through faith—and this not from yourselves, it is the gift of God—not by works, so that no one can boast" (Ephesians 2:4, 8).

So how do we receive this incredible gift? We simply confess and believe.

The Provision

"But God demonstrates his own love for us in this: While we were still sinners, Christ died for us" (Romans 5:8).

All through the Old Testament, men and women realized that they could not meet God's standards for holy living. A cycle of rebellion, judgment, repentance, and revival runs throughout Israel's history. And don't we see that in our own hearts? I'm so glad that God loves us despite our weaknesses and frailties.

At the perfect time on God's kingdom calendar, He looked at His Son and said, "Now is the time." And on that starry night in Bethlehem, the God-man was born to a virgin named Mary, wrapped in swaddling clothes, and laid in a manger. Smelly sheep, dirty cows, and clucking chickens welcomed the King of kings into the world as the angels sang a symphony of praise heard by common man.

Jesus lived a perfect sinless life, even though He was tempted and tried just as you and I are today. Then Jesus gave His life as a sacrifice and died a cruel death on a Roman cross. He was the last sacrifice required by God, once and for all. But three days later, just as Satan's victory party was in full swing, the almighty power of God raised Jesus from the dead, the stone was rolled away, and the resurrected Christ burst forth in fullness of life.

"You see, at just the right time, when we were still powerless, Christ died for the ungodly [that's you and me]. Very rarely will anyone die for a righteous man, though for a good man someone might possibly dare to die. But God demonstrates his own love for us in this: While we were still sinners, Christ died for us" (Romans 5:6-8).

The Promise

"If you confess with your mouth, 'Jesus is Lord,' and believe in your heart that God raised him from the dead, you will be saved. For it is with your heart that you believe and are justified, and it is with your mouth that you confess and are saved. As the Scripture says, 'Anyone who trusts in him will never be put to shame'" (Romans 10:9-11).

God gives us this promise: If we confess with our mouths and believe in our hearts that God raised Jesus from the dead, we will be saved. There is not a long list of rules to obey, only a Person to follow.

Confession is an outward expression of our inward belief. It is more than simply saying something out loud. Even the demons know that Jesus is the Son of God. Many times in the Bible they acknowledged who He was. *Confession* "is the deep personal conviction, without reservation, that Jesus is that person's own master or sovereign. This phrase includes repenting from sin, trusting in Jesus for salvation, and submitting to Him as Lord."[46] To *confess* is to say the same thing or to be in agreement with someone. When we confess Jesus as Lord, we are agreeing with God's declaration of Jesus' true identity.

As we replace the lies with the truth, there is spiritual power in speaking the truth out loud. Satan is not omniscient. While he can whisper thoughts into your mind, he cannot read your mind. Only God has that ability. So when you confess Jesus as Lord, not only are you confessing it for the world to hear, you are confessing it for the realm of darkness to hear as well.

We confess with our mouths and believe in our hearts. And what are we to believe? Here Paul says, "believe in your heart that God raised him from the dead." Without the resurrection, there would be no salvation. Jesus would be just like every other founder of a major religion who walked the face of the earth—dead. But what makes

Christianity different from all other religions is that our Leader lives. He was resurrected from the dead and lives now at the right hand of the Father praying for you and me.

Salvation through faith has always been God's plan, and no one is excluded from the invitation. As Paul says, "Anyone who trusts in him will never be put to shame" (Romans 10:11).

The Proclamation

"Therefore, there is now no condemnation for those who are in Christ Jesus, because through Christ Jesus the law of the Spirit of life set me free from the law of sin and death" (Romans 8:1).

Imagine standing before a court of law. You've been convicted on multiple counts and the sentencing is about to begin. But just before the judge makes his pronouncement about your punishment, someone walks from the back of the courtroom and approaches the bench.

"Judge, I know that this woman is guilty of every crime brought before the court today. I know that she deserves a life sentence without parole. But I come before you today, in the presence of these witnesses, and offer to serve in her stead. My life for her life so that she may go free."

The judge looks at this man whose eyes are full of compassion and love. "Very well," he says. As the man who redeemed her life is led away in chains, the judge turns to the woman and says, "Not guilty. You are free."

When we come to Christ, all our sins, past, present, and future are forgiven—tossed into the deepest of seas. *Condemnation* is a legal term used to paint a picture of us standing before the Judge in a court of law. Our record has been expunged, wiped clean, and there is therefore now no condemnation for those who are in Christ Jesus. We are accepted by God and adopted as His child.

Just as you could do nothing to earn your salvation, you can do nothing to lose it. Jesus is able to keep those who are entrusted to Him. "To him who is able to keep you from falling and to present you before his glorious presence without fault and with great joy—to the only

God our Savior be glory, majesty, power and authority, through Jesus Christ our Lord, before all ages, now and forevermore! Amen" (Jude 24). While you can do nothing to change your standing as a child of God, there is much you can do to change the state—the closeness of the relationship. Throughout life we ebb and flow, depending on our obedience, in our closeness to God.

Nothing can separate you from the love of God (Romans 8:38-39). But the depth and intimacy of your relationship with Him is proportional to the time you spend with Him reading His Word, talking to Him in prayer, and listening to His still small voice.

Let's say that you met and married the man of your dreams, but soon after you walked the aisle and said "I do," you moved to Texas. He is still in North Carolina, and you call him once a week to tell him what you need. Oh, let's say you call him on Sundays, except when you're too tired to pick up the phone. How much intimacy would you expect from such a union? How well would you know your man?

It's not enough to simply walk the aisle and be joined to your heavenly bridegroom. In order to have an intimate relationship, we must spend time getting to know Him. If not, we will begin to feel distant. I've been married over 25 years and I continue to make new discoveries about my man. Likewise, I've been a Christian for over 30 years, and I'm still making incredible discoveries about my Lord.

The Prayer

"Everyone who calls on the name of the Lord will be saved" (Romans 10:13).

If you can't remember a time when you accepted Jesus as your Savior and Lord, why not clear that up right now. If you have never asked Jesus to be your Lord and Savior and would like to accept that precious gift from God, we can do that today.

Let's pray together.

Dear Heavenly Father, I come to you today as a sinner in need of a

Savior. I confess that I have sinned and made many mistakes in my life.
I am unable to live a holy life on my own. I believe in my heart that
Jesus Christ is Your Son, who was born of a virgin, lived a perfect life,
and gave Himself as a sacrifice to pay the penalty for my sins. I believe
that He rose from the dead on the third day and now lives forever with
You. I come to You in faith, believing. Thank You for giving me the gift
of eternal life.
  In Jesus' name,
  Amen.

The Lifter of My Head

Karen had done it all. For fourteen years she had maintained a household, a live-in boyfriend, three kids, and a dog. But her heart was so broken. She was lost and felt that she could never be good enough to be a Christian. "I could never feel comfortable walking into a church," she said. "Besides, I didn't want to stop partying. Cussing was my first language, and I didn't think I could ever be any different."

One day Karen's cousin asked her to go with her to a small group Bible study. "I don't want to go by myself," the cousin said. "Please go with me."

So Karen put on her happy face and went along. The more she learned about God, the worse she felt. But the women seemed to have a joy she didn't have. For the first time she saw that there might be hope for her. She saw the light in the ladies' eyes and wanted that for herself. God was calling her.

"I was not a good person," Karen said. "I can't even begin to tell you all the things that I had done. And all the things I'd have to change? Oh, my. There was so much. I tried to shut God out, but the more I prayed, the more He revealed Himself to me.

"Finally, at the end of several long hard months, I came to Him. I knew I could not be all that God wanted me to be, but I was so desperate. With my head hanging down (it seems like my head was always hanging down), I started to pray. I felt God surround me with a peace I had never known. Then He gently said, 'Lift your head. You are My daughter, and I love you.'

"I poured out my heart to Jesus that day. He knew upfront what I was like, and He still wanted me. My life has never been the same. I still have struggles, but God is there to see me through.

"I accepted Christ in March 2006, my seven-year-old son asked Jesus into his heart the summer of 2007, and my boyfriend and I got married a few months after that. While once I couldn't bring myself to go to church, now I can't stay away. God is my lifeline, and it all started with a few women in a small Bible study just trying to help each other learn about God."

Karen thought she would never be good enough to be a Christian, but God, the lifter of her head, told her Jesus had already been good enough for her.

It's All About Him

Steve and I boarded a cog train for a scenic ride to the top of Pike's Peak near Colorado Springs. It is the most visited mountain in North America—a hiker's paradise. But since going up and down my stairs at home is about as much hiking as I like to do, we opted for the train to chug us to the top. This stately mountain stands as a majestic backdrop to Colorado Springs and the Garden of the Gods rock formations. As we clicked along the 8.9 miles of railway, a tour guide pointed out various interests and wildlife along the way. Suddenly, the train slowed to a crawl and a chorus of *ooohs* and *aaahs* resounded through the cars. In hushed silence, we gazed at a herd of bighorn sheep to our right.

Rams with white fluffy rumps gathered in a circle like spectators at a boxing match. Two rams stood head-to-head in the center of the ring, eyeing each other with studied determination. Smaller ewes with diminutive spiked horns grazed nearby. It seems it was mating season, and the males were vying for the ladies' attention.

A loud *crack* filled the air as the two males ran toward each other and butted heads. Time and time again the males butted heads with one thing on their minds—the right to mate with the seemingly disinterested females. (Oh, we ladies can be so coy at times.)

After viewing this incredible display of God's creation, we broke out in cheers as the train continued its trek up the mountain. The tour guide enthusiastically shouted, "Folks, give yourselves a big hand. I've never seen such a display on any of my trips up the mountain. Give yourselves a round of applause for seeing this magnificent sight today." The entire coach broke out in wild cheers and applause. Well, not the entire coach.

I looked at Steve and said, "Why in the world would we give ourselves a hand? Why are these people clapping? We had absolutely nothing to do with it. God placed that in front of us for our enjoyment. He allowed a sneak peek at His divine creation. All we did was decide to get on the train."

Then I heard God speak to my heart. *Happens all the time.*

Oh dear friend, God has given us an incredible gift of salvation. We don't earn it, merit it, or deserve it. If we did, it would not be a gift. Salvation is not something we should congratulate ourselves for. We have nothing to do with it. All we did was decide to get on the train. But praise God, He has promised us the ride of our lives filled with incredible displays of His splendor.

We don't have to earn it. We simply have to accept it. And what an exciting life we will have.

● ● ● **Recognize the lie:** I'm not good enough to be a Christian.

● ● ● **Reject the lie:** That is not true.

● ● ● **Replace the lie with truth:**

- "But when the kindness and love of God our Savior appeared, he saved us, not because of righteous things we had done, but because of his mercy" (Titus 3:4-5).

- "He is able to save completely those who come to God through him, because he always lives to intercede for them" (Hebrews 7:25).

- "For God so loved the world that he gave his one and only Son, that whoever believes in him shall not perish but have eternal life" (John 3:16).

- "[Jesus said], 'No one can snatch them out of my Father's hand'" (John 10:29).

Second Glances

Carrie stood before the bathroom mirror putting the finishing touches on her makeup before rushing off to the county fair with her girlfriends. It had been ten years since she and the old gang had ventured to the traveling carnival. A lot had happened since then. Some good. Some bad. But through all the joys and trials of the past decade, Carrie had come to know Jesus. She had traded in her religion for an intimate relationship with God.

I'm so thankful for Mary Marshall, Carrie thought. *She opened my eyes to the truth of who I am as a child of God. I no longer believe the enemy's lies that I'm not good enough, that I'm worthless, or that I'm a failure. Oh, I am so thankful for the truth of Jesus that has set me free from the bondage of the lies. No more shame!*

The honking horn interrupted Carrie's thoughts. She grabbed her sweater and yelled to her mom still in the kitchen. She kissed each of her kids goodbye and ran for the door before they started begging her to stay.

"Bye mom, I'll be home by eleven," Carrie said.

"Be careful," her mom called out.

Carrie, Katie, Clair, and Meghan scurried from booth to booth as the carnival barkers drew them in. They laughed at a new crop of teenage boys who tried to prove their manhood by banging hammers, firing rifles, and shooting hoops. The girls tried their hand at the old games and laughed as they stuck their fingers in the water to pick up ducks. They even reminisced with clouds of sticky cotton candy that melted on contact.

"Come one, come all," the barker called. "Step right up and see yourself as you've never been seen before. The House of Mirrors, sure to entertain and amuse. Step right up."

"Come on in, little lady," the dark man with greasy black hair and toothy grin motioned to Carrie. She shivered and wanted to turn and run way.

"Let's go in here," Katie said. "This'll be fun."

Carrie was whisked away with the crowd and lured into the first mirrored room. Elongated reflections stared back, and the girls giggled at the older, taller, thinner versions of themselves. In the next room, they laughed at their stubby arms and legs and wondered where the mirrors were that took away wrinkles.

The girls then ran to a third room, but Carrie stayed behind. She was silent as she stared at what she saw staring back at her. Words began to appear across her chest, fading in and out in various scripted forms. *Deeply loved. Completely forgiven. Fully pleasing. Priceless treasure. Accepted. New creation. Chosen. Holy. Valuable. Redeemed. Cleansed. Free.*

She couldn't move. She couldn't breathe.

Tears of joy trickled down Carrie's smiling face. "Thank you, God, for opening my eyes to the truth. I love You so much."

As she ran to catch up with the others, everyone noticed a special glow that glistened from her tear-streaked face...they always did.

Replacing the Lies with the Truth Quick Reference Guide

••• **LIE:** I'm not good enough.

••• **TRUTH:** Because of Jesus Christ and His work of redemption, I am deeply loved, completely forgiven, fully pleasing, and totally accepted by God. I am empowered and equipped by the Holy Spirit to do all God has called me to do.

> *"But you were washed, you were sanctified, you were justified in the name of the Lord Jesus Christ and by the Spirit of our God"* *(1 Corinthians 6:11).*

••• **LIE:** I'm not smart enough.

••• **TRUTH:** I have the mind of Christ.

> *"But we have the mind of Christ"* *(1 Corinthians 2:16).*

••• **LIE:** I'm rejected.

••• **TRUTH:** I have been chosen.

> *"For he chose us in him before the creation of the world"* *(Ephesians 1:4).*

••• **LIE:** I'm condemned.

••• **TRUTH:** I am forgiven.

> *"If we confess our sins, he is faithful and just and will forgive us our sins and purify us from all unrighteousness" (1 John 1:9).*

••• **LIE:** I'm a loser.

••• **TRUTH:** I am a conqueror.

> *"In all these things we are more than conquerors through him who loved us" (Romans 8:37).*

••• **LIE:** I'm insecure.

••• **TRUTH:** I am secure.

> *"Those who fear the LORD are secure" (Proverbs 14:26 NLT).*

••• **LIE:** I'm inadequate.

••• **TRUTH:** My adequacy is in Christ.

> *"Not that we are adequate in ourselves to consider anything as coming from ourselves, but our adequacy is from God" (2 Corinthians 3:5 NASB).*

••• **LIE:** I'm inferior. I'm just a nobody.

••• **TRUTH:** I am a child of the King.

> *"Yet to all who received him, to those who believed in his name, he gave the right to become children of God" (John 1:12).*

••• **LIE:** I'm insignificant. I don't matter to anyone.

••• **TRUTH:** I am God's child.

> *"How great is the love the Father has lavished on us, that we should be called children of God! And that is what we are!" (1 John 3:1).*

••• **LIE:** I'm incompetent. I can't do anything right.

••• **TRUTH:** I am competent and empowered by the Holy Spirit.

> *"Not that we are competent in ourselves to claim anything for ourselves, but our competence comes from God. He has made us competent as ministers of a new covenant" (2 Corinthians 3:5-6).*

••• **LIE:** I'm incomplete. I need _____ to be fulfilled.

••• **TRUTH:** I have been made complete in Christ.

> *"For in Him dwells all the fullness of the Godhead bodily; and you are complete in Him, who is the head of all principality and power" (Colossians 2:9-10 NKJV).*

••• **LIE:** I'm unacceptable.

••• **TRUTH:** I am totally accepted by God.

> *"Accept one another, then, just as Christ accepted you, in order to bring praise to God" (Romans 15:7).*

••• **LIE:** I'm all alone.

••• **TRUTH:** God and His heavenly angels are always with me.

> *"The angel of the LORD encamps around those who fear him, and he delivers them" (Psalm 34:7).*

••• **LIE:** I can't do anything right.

••• **TRUTH:** I can do all things through Christ who strengthens me.

> *"I can do everything through him who gives me strength" (Philippians 4:13).*

••• **LIE:** I'm worthless.

••• **TRUTH:** The Lord has chosen me to be His treasured possession. My worth is not based on what others think of me, but on what God thinks of me...and He thinks I'm priceless.

> *"Out of all the peoples on the face of the earth, the LORD has chosen you to be his treasured possession" (Deuteronomy 14:2).*

••• **LIE:** I'm helpless.

••• **TRUTH:** God is my strength.

> *"Fear not, for I am with you. Do not be dismayed. I am your God. I will strengthen you; I will help you; I will uphold you with My victorious right hand...I am holding you by your right hand—I, the Lord your God—and I say to you, Don't be afraid; I am here to help you" (Isaiah 41:10,13 TLB).*

••• **LIE:** I will never figure this out.

••• **TRUTH:** God will give me wisdom.

> *"Whether you turn to the right or to the left, your ears will hear a voice behind you, saying, 'This is the way; walk in it'" (Isaiah 30:21).*

> *"If any of you lacks wisdom, he should ask God, who gives generously to all without finding fault, and it will be given to him" (James 1:5).*

••• **LIE:** I'm a bad person.

••• **TRUTH:** I am a partaker of God's divine nature.

> *"Through these [everything we need for life and godliness] he has given us his very great and precious promises, so that through them you may participate in the divine nature and escape the corruption in the world caused by evil desires" (2 Peter 1:4).*

••• **LIE:** My sin is unforgivable.

••• **TRUTH:** God has forgiven me of all my sins.

"If we confess our sins, he is faithful and just and will forgive us our sins and purify us from all unrighteousness" (1 John 1:9).

• • • **LIE:** I'm used goods.

• • • **TRUTH:** I am a new creation—God's temple.

> *"Therefore, if anyone is in Christ he is a new creation; the old has gone, the new has come!" (2 Corinthians 5:17).*

> *"Don't you know that you yourselves are God's temple and that God's Spirit lives in you?" (1 Corinthians 3:16).*

• • • **LIE:** I'm powerless.

• • • **TRUTH:** I have been given the power of the Holy Spirit.

> *"I pray also that the eyes of your heart may be enlightened in order that you may know...his incomparably great power for us who believe" (Ephesians 1:18-19).*

• • • **LIE:** I'm an outcast.

• • • **TRUTH:** I have been adopted into God's family.

> *"In love he predestined us to be adopted as his sons through Jesus Christ" (Ephesians 1:5).*

• • • **LIE:** I'm weak.

• • • **TRUTH:** I am strong in the Lord. His power is working in me.

> *"The LORD is the strength of my life" (Psalm 27:1 NKJV).*

• • • **LIE:** I'm condemned.

• • • **TRUTH:** I am forgiven.

> *"Therefore, there is now no condemnation for those who are in Christ Jesus" (Romans 8:1).*

• • • **Lie:** I'm all alone.

• • • **Truth:** Jesus is always with me.

> *"God has said, 'Never will I leave you; never will I forsake you'"*
> *(Hebrews 13:5).*

> *"Then Jesus came to them and said, '…And surely I am with you*
> *always, to the very end of the age'" (Matthew 28:18,20).*

• • • **Lie:** I'm not safe.

• • • **Truth:** God will protect me.

> *"The name of the LORD is a strong tower; the righteous run to it and*
> *are safe" (Proverbs 18:10).*

• • • **Lie:** I can't take this any longer.

• • • **Truth:** I can endure.

> *"For everyone born of God overcomes the world. This is the victory*
> *that has overcome the world, even our faith" (1 John 5:4-5).*

• • • **Lie:** I can't get past my past.

• • • **Truth:** God makes all things new. I am a new creation.

> *"Therefore, if anyone is in Christ he is a new creation; the old has*
> *gone, the new has come!" (2 Corinthians 5:17).*

• • • **Lie:** I can't resist temptation.

• • • **Truth:** Through the power of the Holy Spirit, I can resist temptation.

> *"Resist the devil and he will flee from you" (James 4:7).*

> *"No temptation has seized you except what is common to man. And*
> *God is faithful; he will not let you be tempted beyond what you can*
> *bear. But when you are tempted, he will also provide a way out so*
> *that you can stand up under it" (1 Corinthians 10:13).*

••• LIE: I can't let anyone know about my past.

••• TRUTH: There is incredible power in my personal story of forgiveness and deliverance. It is the enemy who wants me to keep it quiet.

> *"They overcame [Satan] by the blood of the Lamb and by the word of their testimony" (Revelation 12:11).*

••• LIE: I just can't help myself.

••• TRUTH: I can stop this sinful habit through the power of Christ.

> *"For we know that our old self was crucified with him so that the body of sin might be done away with, that we should no longer be slaves to sin—because anyone who has died has been freed from sin" (Romans 6:6).*

••• LIE: I can't trust God to take care of my needs.

••• TRUTH: I can trust God to take care of my needs.

> *"And my God will meet all your needs according to his glorious riches in Christ Jesus" (Philippians 4:19).*

••• LIE: I don't believe God hears my prayers.

••• TRUTH: God always hears my prayers.

> *"This is the confidence we have in approaching God: that if we ask anything according to his will, he hears us. And if we know that he hears us—whatever we ask—we know that we have what we asked of him" (1 John 5:14-15).*

••• LIE: I don't need God on this one. I can handle this one on my own.

••• TRUTH: I cannot do anything significant apart from Christ working through me.

> *"I am the vine; you are the branches. If a man remains in me and*

I in him, he will bear much fruit; apart from me you can do nothing'" (John 15:5).

••• **LIE:** I don't have what it takes to succeed in life.

••• **TRUTH:** God has given me everything I need to do all He has called me to do.

> *"His divine power has given us everything we need for life and godliness through our knowledge of him who called us by his own glory and goodness"* (2 Peter 1:3).

••• **LIE:** I don't have enough faith.

••• **TRUTH:** God has given me all the faith I need. I simply need to exercise it and believe.

> *"God has allotted to each a measure of faith"* (Romans 12:3 NASB).

> *"I tell you the truth, if you have faith as small as a mustard seed, you can say to this mountain, "Move from here to there" and it will move. Nothing will be impossible for you'"* (Matthew 17:20).

••• **LIE:** I'll never do anything significant with my life.

••• **TRUTH:** God has wonderful plans for my life.

> *"We are God's workmanship, created in Christ Jesus to do good works, which God prepared in advance for us to do"* (Ephesians 2:10).

••• **LIE:** I'll never recover from this horrible circumstance. Life will never be the same.

••• **TRUTH:** God will cause all things to work for good in my life.

> *"And we know that in all things God works for the good of those who love him, who have been called according to his purpose"* (Romans 8:28).

••• LIE: Nobody ever prays for me.

••• TRUTH: Jesus prays for me continually.

> *"Christ Jesus, who died—more than that, who was raised to life—is at the right hand of God and is also interceding for us" (Romans 8:34).*

••• LIE: Nobody knows what I'm going through.

••• TRUTH: Jesus understands what I am going through.

> *"For we do not have a high priest who is unable to sympathize with our weaknesses, but we have one who has been tempted in every way, just as we are—yet was without sin" (Hebrews 4:15).*

••• LIE: Nobody loves me.

••• TRUTH: God loves me greatly.

> *"How great is the love the Father has lavished on us, that we should be called children of God! And that is what we are!" (1 John 3:1).*

••• LIE: God won't forgive me this time.

••• TRUTH: God will forgive me when I confess, repent, and ask.

> *"Because of the LORD's great love we are not consumed, for his compassions never fail. They are new every morning; great is your faithfulness" (Lamentations 3:22-23).*

••• LIE: God is not really good.

••• TRUTH: God is good all the time.

> *"You are good, and what you do is good" (Psalm 119:68).*

••• LIE: God's love for me is related to my performance.

••• TRUTH: God's love for me is not based on my performance but on the finished work of Jesus Christ.

"For it is by grace you have been saved through faith—and this not from yourselves, it is the gift of God—not by works, so that no one can boast" (Ephesians 2:8-9).

• • • **LIE:** God has forgotten me.

• • • **TRUTH:** God will never forget me.

> *"Can a mother forget the baby at her breast and have no compassion on the child she has borne? Though she may forget, I will not forget you! See, I have engraved you on the palms of my hands" (Isaiah 49:15-16).*

• • • **LIE:** God doesn't care about me.

• • • **TRUTH:** God knows the number of hairs on my head and is concerned with every aspect of my life.

> *"And even the very hairs of your head are all numbered. So don't be afraid; you are worth more than many sparrows" (Matthew 10:30-31).*

• • • **LIE:** I have reason to fear.

• • • **TRUTH:** God will protect me. I do not need to be afraid.

> *"I sought the LORD, and He heard me, and delivered me from all my fears" (Psalm 34:4 NKJV).*

• • • **LIE:** I want to obey You, but it's too hard.

• • • **TRUTH** : God will never ask me to do anything that He will not give me the power to do.

> *"What I am commanding you today is not too difficult for you or beyond your reach" (Deuteronomy 30:11).*

• • • **LIE:** I need _____ to feel complete.

••• **Truth:** I am complete in Christ.

> *"For in Him dwells all the fullness of the Godhead bodily; and you are complete in Him, who is the head of all principality and power"* (Colossians 2:9-10 NKJV).

••• **Lie:** My marriage is hopeless.

••• **Truth:** Nothing is impossible for God. He can heal my marriage.

> *"'For nothing is impossible for God'"* (Luke 1:37).

••• **Lie:** My finances are hopeless.

••• **Truth:** God can take care of my finances if I seek Him first.

> *"But seek first his kingdom and his righteousness, and all these things will be given to you as well"* (Matthew 6:33).

••• **Lie:** I've really blown it this time. God will never love me again.

••• **Truth:** There is nothing I could do to make God not love me.

> *"For I am convinced that neither death not life, neither angels nor demons, neither the present nor the future, nor any powers, neither height nor depth, nor anything else in all creation, will be able to separate us from the love of God that is in Christ Jesus our Lord"* (Romans 8:38-39).

••• **Lie:** It's my body. I can do what I want.

••• **Truth:** My body is God's temple.

> *"Do you not know that your body is a temple of the Holy Spirit, who is in you, whom you have received from God? You are not your own; you were bought at a price. Therefore honor God with your body"* (1 Corinthians 6:19).

••• **Lie:** He's not a Christian, but I'm going to marry him anyway. I'm sure it will all work out.

••• **TRUTH:** God has commanded believers not to marry unbelievers.

> *"Do not be yoked together with unbelievers. For what do righteousness and wickedness have in common?...What does a believer have in common with an unbeliever?" (2 Corinthians 6:14,15).*

••• **LIE:** I deserve better.

••• **TRUTH:** I deserve hell. God doesn't owe me anything. I owe Him everything.

> *"Do nothing out of selfish ambition or vain conceit, but in humility consider others better than yourselves...Your attitude should be the same as that of Christ Jesus: Who, being in very nature God, did not consider equality with God something to be grasped, but made himself nothing, taking the very nature of a servant, being made in human likeness" (Philippians 2:3,5-7).*

••• **LIE:** The devil made me do it.

••• **TRUTH:** The devil can't make me do anything.

> *"The one who is in you is greater than the one who is in the world"* (1 John 4:4).

••• **LIE:** I'd be happy if I just had _____.

••• **TRUTH:** My joy comes from knowing God.

> *"I have learned to be content whatever the circumstances" (Philippians 4:11).*

••• **LIE:** I have to pay for my sins.

••• **TRUTH:** Jesus paid for my sins.

> *"'Just as the Son of Man did not come to be served, but to serve, and to give his life as a ransom for many'" (Matthew 20:28).*

••• **LIE:** It's my life. I can do what I want.

••• **TRUTH:** My life now belongs to God.

> *"You were bought at a price. Therefore honor God with your body"*
> *(1 Corinthians 6:20).*

••• **LIE:** I have no purpose in life.

••• **TRUTH:** God has great plans for my life.

> *"No eye has seen, no ear has heard, no mind has conceived what God*
> *has prepared for those who love him" (1 Corinthians 2:9).*

••• **LIE:** This problem is too big. It cannot be fixed.

••• **TRUTH:** No problem is too difficult for God.

> *"O Sovereign Lord! You made the heavens and earth by your strong*
> *hand and powerful arm. Nothing is too hard for you!" (Jeremiah*
> *32:17 NLT).*

••• **LIE:** I should be worried.

••• **TRUTH:** I don't need to be worried. God is in control.

> *"Do not be anxious about anything, but in everything, by prayer and*
> *petition, with thanksgiving, present your requests to God. And the*
> *peace of God, which transcends all understanding, will guard your*
> *hearts and your minds in Christ Jesus" (Philippians 4:6-7).*

••• **LIE:** I feel dirty.

••• **TRUTH:** I have been cleansed and made pure and holy.

> *"But you were washed, you were sanctified, you were justified in*
> *the name of the Lord Jesus Christ and by the Spirit of our God"*
> *(1 Corinthians 6:11).*

••• **LIE:** God doesn't hear my prayers.

••• **TRUTH:** God hears my every prayer.

> *"The LORD is near to all who call on him, to all who call on him in truth. He fulfills the desires of those who fear him; he hears their cry and saves them" (Psalm 145:18-19).*

••• **LIE:** God could never use me.

••• **TRUTH:** God can and will use me to accomplish His purposes for my life.

> *"'You did not choose me, but I chose you and appointed you to go and bear fruit—fruit that will last'" (John 15:16).*

••• **LIE:** If someone doesn't like me, then something is wrong with me.

••• **TRUTH:** Not everyone will like me. Not everyone liked Jesus.

> *"He was despised and rejected by men, a man of sorrows, and familiar with suffering" (Isaiah 53:3).*

••• **LIE:** I can dress the way I want. If a man is tempted, that's his problem.

••• **TRUTH:** I must not dress in a way that causes a brother to be tempted.

> *"Do not cause anyone to stumble" (1 Corinthians 10:32).*

••• **LIE:** I can't trust God to take care of me.

••• **TRUTH:** I can trust God to take care of me.

> *"'Therefore I tell you, do not worry about your life, what you will eat or drink; or about your body, what you will wear...But seek first his kingdom and his righteousness, and all these things will be given to you as well'" (Matthew 6:25,33).*

••• **LIE:** I need _____ to be happy and secure.

••• **TRUTH:** My happiness and security come from knowing Jesus.

> *"Because the Lord is my Shepherd, I have everything I need!" (Psalm 23:1 TLB).*

••• **LIE:** I used to be a Christian, but I lost my salvation.

••• **TRUTH:** I did not do anything to earn my salvation. It is all about what Jesus did, not what I do. Therefore, I cannot lose my salvation because of poor performance.

> *[Jesus said,] 'I give them eternal life, and they shall never perish; no one can snatch them out of my hand'" (John 10:28).*

••• **LIE:** I have rights.

••• **TRUTH:** The way to joy is to lay down my rights.

> *"Your attitude should be the same as that of Christ Jesus: Who, being in very nature God, did not consider equality with God something to be grasped, but made himself nothing, taking the very nature of a servant, being made in human likeness" (Philippians 2:5-7).*

Bible Study Guide

This Bible study guide is designed to enhance the message of *"I'm Not Good Enough"...and Other Lies Women Tell Themselves.* The lessons do not coincide with particular chapters in the book, but are written to help cement the truth in our minds and bring great victory in our lives. Let's get started.

Lesson One: The Enemy's Demise

1. Before Jesus began His earthly ministry, God wanted to make sure the world knew exactly who Jesus was and just how His heavenly Father felt about Him. Read Luke 3:15-22 and note what God said when Jesus came up out of the water.

2. God has great plans for you. Did you know that? Read 1 Corinthians 2:9. But before we can accomplish all that God wants us to accomplish and be all that God wants us to be, we have to know who we are. Read 1 John 3:1 and fill in the blanks. I am God's _____, whom He _____.

3. Right after Jesus was baptized; the Holy Spirit led Him into the desert to be tempted by Satan. Satan knew exactly who Jesus was and why He came. In the wilderness he challenged Jesus, as if to say, "If you are God's Son, then prove it."

What were the three temptations recorded in Luke 4:1-13 and how did Jesus preface each answer?

4. In Chapter 2, we took a look at the enemy's true identity. Read Ezekiel 28:12-17 and Isaiah 14:12-15 and list everything you learn about Satan's fall.

Bible scholars have long pondered these verses, and it is uncertain whether they point specifically to Satan's fall from heaven or simply to earthly kings. One commentator wrote: "Nothing could be more appropriate, for the pride of the king of Babylon was truly satanic. When Satan works his malign will through rulers of this word, he reproduces his own wicked qualities in them, so that they become virtual shadows of which he is the substance."[47] Whether it is written about Satan or earthly kings, Satan was pulling the puppets' strings.

5. Look up the following verses and note what you learn about Satan and how he works.

   a. John 8:44

   b. 2 Corinthians 4:4

   c. 2 Corinthians 11:14

   d. Ephesians 6:11-12

   e. 1 Peter 5:8

6. Look up in a dictionary the following words that the Bible uses to describe the enemy and note what you learn about the enemy's tactics. Give an example of each one.

   a. Murderer (John 8:44)

   b. Deceiver (2 Corinthians 11:14)

   c. Accuser (Revelation 12:10)

   d. Liar (John 8:44)

7. According to the following verses, what did Jesus come to do?

   a. 1 John 3:8

   b. John 10:10

   c. Luke 4:18-19

8. I know we're only at the beginning of this study, but I have great faith that we're going to experience incredible victory. So rather than wait until the last lesson together, let's go ahead and start the party. Read the following verses and note what you learn about the victory we have in Jesus.

   a. 1 Corinthians 15:57

   b. 2 Corinthians 2:14

   c. 1 John 5:4

Let's close today's lesson in prayer:

> *Dear Heavenly Father, thank You that Jesus came to overcome the work of the devil in our lives. Help us to understand and be empowered by the truth of Your Word. We celebrate the victory we have through Jesus Christ, our Lord. In Jesus' name, amen.*

Lesson Two: Living in Confidence

1. The enemy will do everything he can to keep us from going where God wants us to go and doing what God wants us to do. Read Mark 4:35-41 and answer the following questions:

   a. Describe what happened while Jesus was sleeping.

   b. Describe the disciples' emotional state—fear or calm?

   c. Describe Jesus' emotional state—fear or calm?

   d. What did the disciples say to Jesus when they woke Him up?

   e. Have you ever said that to God? Be honest.

   f. What did Jesus do, and how did He do it?

   g. What did He say to the disciples?

Jesus is concerned with every aspect of our lives, and He wants us to believe that He can still calm the storms. Do you have a storm in your life that needs calming today? Is your emotional state fear or calm? What do you think Jesus is saying to you through this story?

2. Now read a little further. What happened in Mark 5:1-20? Consider the storm. Who do you think would not have wanted Jesus to reach the other side?

   How did Jesus speak to both the storm and the demons?

3. We never need to be afraid of the enemy. He is a toothless lion with a big growl. What does Paul tell us about our approach to our opponents? (Philippians 1:28) What is the reason for this confidence? (1 John 4:4)

4. Not only is Jesus in us, but we are surrounded by a host of angels. Read the following verses and note what you learn.

   a. Hebrews 1:14

   b. 2 Kings 6:15-17

5. What did Jesus pray for you and for me? (John 17:15-21)

6. Just as with Eve, Satan attacks us with lies that tempt us to sin. Can you think of a time you believed the lie and sinned against God?

   a. As with Eve, Satan makes temptation seem appealing. Can you think of some avenues that Satan uses to affect the minds of women in our culture? (For example: television programs, magazines.)

   b. King David didn't have a television, but he certainly watched a "movie" from his rooftop one balmy evening. How might he have avoided falling into Satan's trap and the sin that followed? (2 Samuel 11:1-5)

   c. Is there any area of your life where you are making yourself vulnerable by exposing yourself to lies? Is there anything that you need to change?

7. God doesn't place restrictions on us to keep us from having fun. He gives us guidelines so we can have abundant fulfilling

lives. Read John 10:10 again. How would you describe abundant life?

8. Did you know that God wants to bless you? Read the following and note what you learn about God's heart to bless your life.

    a. Psalm 84:11

    b. 2 Chronicles 16:9

    c. James 1:17

Lesson Three: Tightening the Belt of Truth

1. Read Ephesians 6:10-18 and list the pieces of the armor and what they were used for.

2. In those days, soldiers wore loose-fitting tunics (picture a big sheet with armholes). The belt pulled all the loose ends together and held the tunic close. How does truth pull all the loose ends of our lives together and prepare us for battle?

3. How is God described in the following verses?

    a. Psalm 31:5

    b. Isaiah 65:16

    c. Numbers 23:19

4. How is Jesus described in the following verses?

    a. John 1:14

    b. John 1:17

    c. John 14:6

5. How is the Holy Spirit described in the following verses?

    a. John 14:15-17

    b. John 16:13

6. Read the following verses and note how living in the truth affects your life. Give an example of each.

    a. Psalm 40:11

    b. Psalm 43:3

    c. John 8:32

    d. John 8:51

7. What did David pray in regard to the truth?

    a. Psalm 25:4-5

    b. Psalm 26:2-3

    c. Psalm 51:6

    What are our inner parts?

8. Pilate asked an important question just before Jesus was sentenced to death (John 18:38). Suppose someone asked you that same question. How would you respond?

9. Now, let's go back up to question 2. How does the belt of truth hold our lives together? What happens when we do not have the belt of truth fastened securely in place?

In closing, let's pray God's Word back to Him and join David on his knees.

> *Dear Heavenly Father, show me Your ways, teach me Your paths and guide me in Your truth. Test me, O Lord, and try me, examine my heart and my mind to see if I am believing the lies in any part of my life so that I can have truth in the inner parts of my being: my mind, will, and emotions. In Jesus' name, amen.*

Lesson Four: Holding up the Shield of Faith

1. Go back and read Ephesians 6:10-18 and note once again the pieces of the spiritual armor we are to wear every day. What was

the purpose of the shield? How does faith in God's truth protect us from the lies that Satan shoots?

2. The shields were often covered with leather and soaked in water. When a fiery dart hit the waterlogged shield, it was extinguished on contact. What is water compared to in the following verses?

   a. Ephesians 5:26

   b. John 4:10-13

   How can soaking our lives or immersing ourselves in God's Word help extinguish the fiery lies of the enemy?

3. Look up Hebrews 11:1 and note the definition of *faith*. Now paraphrase that in your own words. What does faith look like in your own life?

4. The Greek words for *faith* and *believe* are closely connected. *Pisteuo* is translated *believe*. It is a verb. *Pistis* is translated *faith*. It is a noun. How are these two words different and how are they similar? Can you have one without the other?

5. What kept the Israelites out of the Promised Land? (Numbers 13:17–14:35; note especially 14:11) Is there any unbelief in your life that could be keeping you out of your own Promised Land?

   a. Do you see how saying, "I'm not good enough," is believing a lie rather than the truth? Could your unbelief in regards to what you believe about yourself be keeping you out of your Promised Land?

   b. Have you believed an evil report or have you, like Caleb and Joshua, believed God?

6. Our faith is made stronger by confessing what we know. Read the following and note what the writers knew to be true. How would each of these truths combat particular lies?

   a. Romans 8:28

   b. 2 Timothy 1:12

   c. James 1:2-3

   d. 1 Peter 1:18-19

   e. 1 John 4:13

   f. 1 John 4:16

   g. 1 John 5:18-20

We have two mini-shields at the ends of our arms. The next time you hear a lie, either audibly or in your mind, reject it. Hold up your hand as if blocking the lie and say, "That's not true." As my son used to say, "Talk to the hand 'cause the face isn't listening."

Lesson Five: Renewing Your Mind

1. Read Romans 12:2. The word *transformed* implies a process. The moment we accept Jesus Christ as our Lord and Savior, our spirits are instantly changed (2 Corinthians 5:17). However the transformation of the mind, will, and emotions is a process.

2. Read Colossians 3:16. What do you think it means for something to "dwell" in you?

   a. To dwell means to live at a place, to camp out, to think about constantly. How does that relate to dwelling on the truth?

   b. Notice the verse begins with the word "Let." What does that imply about our part in dwelling on the truth?

3. Read Philippians 4:8 and note what we are to dwell on.

4. Go back to Colossians 3:16 and back up a verse to 3:15. What will rule in our hearts when we dwell on the truth?

a. To "rule" means to act as an umpire. How is God's Word like an umpire in our lives? Give some examples.

b. The more time we spend in the truth, the more clearly we can discern God's voice and the more accustomed we grow to detecting the umpire's voice.

5. One way we renew our minds is by meditating on the truth. I think of meditation as mental and spiritual rumination. Read the following and note what you learn about meditation. Especially note what the writer meditated on.

a. Psalm 77:12

b. Psalm 119:15

c. Psalm 119:48

d. Psalm 119:97

e. Psalm 145:5

6. What are the results of meditating on the truth?

a. Proverbs 6:20-22

b. Joshua 1:8-9

c. Psalm 1:2-3

7. Turn to the "Replacing the Lies with the Truth Quick Reference Guide" and pick five lies that you have often believed about yourself. Now write the following on five different index cards:

• *Recognize the lie:* write the lie you have believed.

• *Reject the lie:* write the powerful sentence, "That's not true."

• *Replace the lie with truth:* write the corresponding truth to dispel the lie.

For the next six weeks, meditate on the truth you have recorded.

Put the card in a place you will see often and speak the truth out loud.

8. What is the result of keeping our minds on God's truth (Isaiah 26:3)?

Lesson Six: Speaking the Truth to Your Soul

Some say only crazy people talk to themselves, but I tell you the truth, if I didn't talk to myself I would go crazy. There is something very powerful about the words we speak to ourselves. Let's take a look together at the power of our words to ourselves.

1. Read Romans 10:17. What is made stronger when we *hear* the truth? Don't assume this means when you hear the truth spoken by someone else. It could be when you hear it spoken by yourself to yourself.

2. David talked to himself often. Read the following and note his internal conversations. What did he say to himself?
    a. Psalm 57:8
    b. Psalm 62:5
    c. Psalm 103:1-2, 22

    Do you need to give yourself a good talking to today? If so, try using David's words you've just recorded.

3. Deborah was a prophetess during the times of the judges in the Old Testament. She was God's mouthpiece to the nation, but the Israelites weren't the only people she spoke to.
    a. Read and note what she said in Judges 5:21.
    b. Are there ever times when you need to say those same words to yourself?

4. What two actions are necessary to be saved (Romans 10:9)?

a. How are they different?

b. Who is hearing your confession when you speak it out loud? Once again, this shows the power of the spoken word.

5. What do the following proverbs teach us about the power of our words?

a. Proverbs 12:18

b. Proverbs 18:21

c. Proverbs 21:23

6. From where do our words flow (Luke 6:45)?

My grandmother would say, "What is down in the well will come up in the bucket." How does that relate to Luke 6:45?

7. Our spoken words have more power than our unspoken thoughts. Read Matthew 17:20. What part does speaking play in the exercise of our faith?

8. Read 2 Corinthians 4:13 and fill in the blank.

"I have believed; therefore _____."

What are your words revealing about what you believe?

Lesson Seven: Demolishing Strongholds

For some of us, the lies we have believed have become strongholds in our lives—something we've been holding onto that is now holding onto us. A stronghold can consist of many lies or one deeply engrained lie that has framed how we see ourselves.

1. Read 2 Corinthians 10:3-5. Using your dictionary, define a stronghold. What are the strongholds mentioned in these verses?

What are the weapons we have at our disposal to tear down the strongholds in our lives?

2. If you believe any one of the lies mentioned in this book, they could be a stronghold in your life. Flip to the "Quick Reference Guide" and place a check (in pencil) by any of the lies you believe about yourself. (We're using pencil because I have every confidence that you'll be erasing those checks.)

3. Let's look at a literal stronghold for a moment. All that stood between the Israelites and the Promised Land was a walled city called Jericho. What was God's battle plan for destroying the city walls? (Joshua 6:1-6)

   If you were among the group, do you think you would have been skeptical of such a plan? What was the result of their obedience? (Joshua 6:20-21)

4. Let me ask you again, Is there any lie that you believe about yourself that's keeping you from entering your personal Promised Land? Do you need to march around the lie saying the truth, believing the truth, or even shouting the truth? Go ahead. Give it a try and watch the walls come tumbling down.

5. One of the reasons Jesus came was to set captives free. Read 2 Corinthians 3:17. "Where the Spirit of the Lord is, there is _____."

6. On the Sabbath, Jesus stood up in the synagogue and read Isaiah 61:1-2. What was contained in those verses?

   Then with all eyes on Him, what did He declare? (Luke 4:16).

7. Jesus did set us free from the penalty of sin, but many Christians are still in bondage to strongholds. What does Galatians 5:1 warn against?

   Jesus came to set captives free, no matter what prison has them bound. What is the promise of John 8:32?

Lesson Eight: Recognizing Times of Vulnerability

In this lesson, we'll look at times when we're most vulnerable to believing the lies of the enemy. If he is anything, he is an opportunist with strategic timing.

1. Exhaustion

Skim 1 Kings 18 and note Elijah's incredible victory. Following this great victory, what did Elijah do in 1 Kings 19? What lies of Satan do you think he believed? (1 Kings 19:4-5)

    a. What did God do to refresh and strengthen Elijah?

      After we've had an incredible spiritual encounter with God, we may experience what I call the "Elijah syndrome." Rest, refresh, and don't be surprised if the enemy tries to come with his lies and steal your joy.

    b. What did Jesus tell the disciples to do after a spiritually vigorous day? (Mark 6:31)

2. Wrong Place at the Wrong Time

We've already looked at this passage, but let's review in order to discover times of vulnerability. Read 2 Samuel 11:1-5.

    a. Where was David?

    b. Where was David supposed to be?

    c. How did the enemy take advantage of the situation, and what lies did David believe?

    d. How could David have avoided the temptation in the first place?

Have you ever put yourself in the wrong place and left yourself vulnerable to falling? (Example: a place you should not have been with a person you should not have been with.) How could that have been avoided?

3. Overconfidence in Self

We are also susceptible to the enemy's lies when we're overconfident in our ability to resist them.

Read Mark 14:27-31 and answer the following questions.

  a. What was Jesus' warning to Peter?

  b. What was Peter's reply? (Verses 29,31)

  c. What was the outcome? (Verses 66-72)

Knowing that overconfidence in our own abilities makes us susceptible to attack, how can we pray that God will give us the strength to overcome the evil one on a daily basis?

4. Lack of Knowledge

When Satan tempted Eve with his lies, he tested her to see if she knew the truth. Read Genesis 3:1-3.

  a. What was Eve's response to the serpent's first question?

  b. Was that the truth?

  c. What did the serpent discover by her answer?

  d. What did the psalmist pray in Psalm 119:11?

5. Smack Dab in the Middle of God's Will

We are also vulnerable to the enemy's lies when we're smack dab in the middle of God's will. Read Matthew 4:1-11.

  a. Why did Jesus go into the desert?

  b. What happened while He was there?

  c. How did He fight the enemy's lies?

6. List the five times of greatest vulnerability that we've covered in this lesson. How do we prepare for each of these times of vulnerability?

  a. Ephesians 4:18

b. 1 Peter 4:8

c. 2 Peter 1:3-4

d. Mark 1:35

Lesson Nine: Stopping the Lies

1. God hates lies and He hates it when we tell lies. Do you agree with that statement? Look up the following verses and note what you learn about lying.

   a. Proverbs 6:16-19

   b. Proverbs 12:22

   c. Exodus 20:16

2. When we lie, whose native tongue or language are we speaking? (John 8:44)

3. Look at James 3:9-10. What does it say about praising God and cursing man created in the image of God? Paraphrase James 3:9 in your own words.

   Now, suppose you are cursing yourself...created in God's image. Paraphrase James 3:9-10 in your own words, putting your name in the verse.

4. In the Bible, there are men and women who believed lies about themselves or their situation. We don't always have their exact words, but we can tell by their actions what they believed. Look up the following verses and note what lies you think each person told herself.

   a. Eve (Genesis 3:6)

   b. Sarah (Genesis 16:1,2)

   c. Rebekah (Genesis 25:23 and 27:1-8)

   d. Tamar (2 Samuel 13:12-20)

   e. The widow from Zarephath (1 Kings 17:1-12)

5. There were also women who believed the truth about who they were and the power of God. Read the following and note what truths you think they believed and the result.

    a. Moses' mother (Exodus 2:1-10)

    b. Hannah (1 Samuel 1:9-18)

    c. Mary (Luke 1:26-38)

    d. Mary (John 2:1-5)

    e. The woman with the hemorrhage (Mark 5:25-34)

    f. The Canaanite woman (Matthew 15:22-28)

6. We can pray that God will help us stop lying about ourselves. Read Psalm 139:4 and 141:3 and write a prayer to God.

7. Are you ready to stop telling lies to yourself about yourself? Are you ready to start believing the truth about who you are and who God is? I have to tell you, I am so convicted by this lesson. God has spoken sternly to me about how He feels about me lying... to me...about me. What about you? What has God revealed to you through this lesson?

Lesson Ten: Seeing Yourself as God Sees You

1. Who are you...really? Today, let's take a close look into God's mirror to discover how He sees you. Read the following verses and fill in the blanks.

    a. Matthew 6:26—I am _____

    b. John 14:20—I am _____

    c. John 15:15—I am _____

    d. John 15:16—I am _____

    e. Romans 5:9—I am _____

    f. Romans 8:2—I am _____

    g. Romans 8:17—I am _____

h. Romans 8:27—I am_____

i. Romans 15:7—I am _____

j. 1 Corinthians 3:16—I am _____

k. 1 Corinthians 6:11—I am _____

l. 2 Corinthians 5:17—I am _____

m. Galatians 4:7—I am_____

n. Ephesians 1:11—I am _____

2. Read the following verses and note what you have in Christ.

a. Proverbs 3:26—I have _____

b. John 14:20—I have _____

c. 1 Corinthians 2:16—I have _____

d. 2 Corinthians 1:22-23—I have _____

e. Ephesians 2:17-18—I have _____

f. Philippians 4:13—I have _____

3. One of the key themes of Ephesians is that we are "in Christ." We often hear about having Jesus in us, but for every time the Bible says Jesus is in us, there are 10 that say we are in Jesus. Skim through Ephesians and list a few of the verses that say we are "in Christ." Look for pronouns such as he or him.

4. When we think of Jesus in us, we think of Jesus going wherever we go. Now, when you think of you in Jesus, what picture do you see?

Lesson Eleven: The One Jesus Loves

1. I hope you are getting a better picture of who you really are. Let's look at one of my favorite passages, Ephesians 1:3-8, and list eight words that describe your identity in Christ.

2. Did you know that God is crazy about you? The apostle John knew that Jesus loved him. How did he refer to himself in his gospel? (John 13:23; 19:26; 21:7, 20)

That's how you can begin introducing yourself. Let's give it a try. I am _____ (your name goes here), the one Jesus loves.

Your heavenly Father has so much planned for you. He has big dreams for your life. But He is waiting for you to put away the lies, to start seeing yourself as He sees you, and to walk in the confidence of a woman who knows she is deeply loved, completely forgiven, fully pleasing, and totally accepted by God. You are empowered and equipped by the Holy Spirit to do all God has called you to do.

3. This lesson is short. I want you to go back to the "Quick Reference" guide and look at the lies you checked earlier. Can you erase them now? I hope so.

4. Take the rest of this time of study today and write what you have learned about the lies you've been telling yourself and the truth that has set you free.

Endnotes

1. Dr. Lynda Hunter, *Who Am I Really?* (Nashville: Word Publishing, 2001), 30.

2. I have gone into great detail about what we lost in the Garden of Eden and what we gained in the Garden of Gethsemane in the book, *Experience the Ultimate Makeover: Discovering God's Transforming Power* (Eugene, OR: Harvest House Publishers, 2007). I encourage you to read that step-by-step explanation of the incredible transformation that occurred in you the moment you believed.

3. Neil Anderson, *Living Free in Christ* (Ventura, CA: Regal Books, 1993), 124.

4. John MacArthur, *The MacArthur Bible Commentary* (Nashville: Thomas Nelson Publishers, 2005), 1704.

5. Francis Frangipane, *The Three Battlegrounds* (Marion, IA: River of Life Ministries, 1989), 36.

6. Robert McGee, *Search for Significance* (Tulsa, OK: Rapha Publishing, 1990), 155.

7. William Backus and Marie Chapian, *Telling Yourself the Truth* (Minneapolis: Bethany House Publishers, 2000), 31.

8. Elizabeth George, *Loving God with All Your Mind* (Eugene, OR: Harvest House Publishers, 1994), 15.

9. www.airsafe.com/events/celebs/jfk_jr.htm

10. www.airlinesafety.com/editorials/JFKJrCrash.htm (Eric Nolte, "Heart Over Mind: The Death of JFK, Jr.").

11. Ibid.

12. Markus Barth, Ephesians 4-6, *The Anchor Bible,* vol. 34A (Garden City, NY: Doubleday, 1974), 763.

13. MacArthur, *MacArthur Bible Commentary*, 1706.

14. Ibid., 1643.

15. Sharon Jaynes, *Extraordinary Moments with God* (Eugene: OR: Harvest House Publishers, 2008), 50-51.

16. *Inspiring Quotations, Contemporary and Classical,* comp. Albert M. Wells, Jr. (Nashville: Thomas Nelson Publishers, 1988), 209.

17. Paul Meier, "Spiritual and Mental Health in the Balance," in *Renewing Your Mind in a Secular World,* ed. John E. Woodbridge (Chicago: Moody Press, 1985), 26-28.

18. Anabel Gillham, *The Confident Woman: Knowing Who You Are in Christ* (Eugene, OR: Harvest House Publishers, 1993), 26-29.

19. Beth Moore, *The Beloved Disciple* (Nashville: LifeWay Press, 2002), 87.

20. Bruce Wilkinson, *The Prayer of Jabez Devotional* (Sisters, OR: Multnomah Publishers, 2001), 62-63.

21. Joann C. Webster and Karen Davis, eds., *A Celebration of Women* (Southlake, TX: Watercolor Books, 2001), 167.

22. Over two-thirds of the world can neither read nor write, so the playback unit allows the tribal people to be discipled by listening to the New Testament in their native tongue. It runs off solar power and will play the New Testament 1,000 times. For more on these two incredible ministries see www.jesusfilm.org and www.faithcomesbyhearing.com.

23. Nick's quotes are taken from *The Hour of Power* television broadcast http://www.crystalcathedral.org/hour_of_power/videos/nick.php. To learn more about Nick Vujicic and his ministry, visit www.lifewithoutlimbs.org

24. Brennan Manning, *Abba's Child: The Cry of the Heart for Intimate Belonging* (Colorado Springs: NavPress, 1994), 26.

25. Source unknown, *Chicken Soup for the Soul,* eds. Jack Cranfield and Mark Hansen (Deerfield Beach, FL: Health Communications, 1993), 237.

26. Chick Moorman, coauthor with Thomas Haller of *Teaching the Attraction Principle to Children* (Merrill, MI: Personal Power Press, 2008). Used by permission of the author. www.chickmoorman.com.

27. Moore, *Beloved Disciple,* 141.

28. Anderson, *Living Free in Christ,* 110.

29. Corrie ten Boom, *Tramp for the Lord* (Grand Rapids: Fleming H. Revell, 1974), 83-86.

30. Diane Dempsey Marr, *The Reluctant Traveler* (Colorado Springs: NavPress, 2002), 113.

31. Spiros Zodhiates et al., eds., *The Complete Word Study Dictionary: New Testament* (Chattanooga, TN: AMG Publishers, 1992), 229.

32. Beth Moore, *Living Beyond Yourself* (Nashville: LifeWay Press: 1998), 120.

33. Beth Moore, *Get Out of that Pit* (Nashville: Thomas Nelson Publishers, 2007), 33-34.

34. Sharon Jaynes, *Your Scars Are Beautiful to God* (Eugene, OR: Harvest House Publishers, 2006), 90-92.

35. Shannon Woodward, *Inconceivable* (Colorado Springs: Cook Communications Ministries, 2006), 9.

36. Linda J. Waite and Maggie Gallagher, *The Case for Marriage* (New York: Doubleday, 2000), 148.

37. Judith Wallerstein, Julia Lewis, and Sandra Blakeslee, *The Unexpected Legacy of Divorce* (New York: Hyperion, 2000), 295.

38. Ibid., 310.

39. Eric Weiner, *The Geography of Bliss* (New York: Twelve, Hachette Book Group USA, 2008), 76.

40. C.S. Lewis, *The Silver Chair* (New York: Macmillan Publishing Company, 1953), 15-17.

41. Woodward, *Inconceivable,* 11.

42. *Random House Unabridged Dictionary,* 2nd ed. (New York: Random House, 1992), s.v. "worry."

43. James Dobson, *When God Doesn't Make Sense* (Wheaton, IL: Tyndale House Publishers, 1993), 8.

44. Woodward, *Inconceivable,* 17.

45. Ibid., 151-54.

46. MacArthur, *MacArthur Bible Commentary,* 1539.

47. *Zondervan NIV Bible Commentary, Volume 1: Old Testament,* ed. Kenneth L. Barker and John R. Kohlenberger III (Grand Rapids: Zondervan, 1994), 1070.

About the Author

Sharon Jaynes is an international inspirational speaker and Bible teacher for women's conferences and events. She is the author of several books including *Becoming the Woman of His Dreams, The Power of a Woman's Words, Your Scars Are Beautiful to God, Experience the Ultimate Makeover,* and *Becoming a Woman Who Listens to God.* Her books have been translated into several foreign languages and impact women around the globe.

Sharon is the cofounder of Girlfriends in God, a conference and on-line ministry that crosses denominational, racial, and generational boundaries to unify the Body of Christ. To learn more visit www.girlfriendsinGod.com.

Sharon and her husband, Steve, have one grown son, Steven. They call North Carolina home.

Sharon is always honored to hear from her readers. You can contact her directly at Sharon@sharonjaynes.com or at her mailing address:

Sharon Jaynes
PO Box 725
Matthews, NC 28106

To learn more about Sharon's books and speaking ministry or to inquire about having her speak at your next event, visit www.sharonjaynes.com.

More Great Harvest House Books
by Sharon Jaynes

YOUR SCARS ARE
BEAUTIFUL TO GOD

Physical scars represent a story, a moment in your life, and they show others there is a history and a healing. Your internal scars—invisible marks from heartbreak, mistakes, and losses—also represent stories of healing and restoration. Author Sharon Jaynes' gentle insight will help you give your wounds to the One who sees your beauty and who can turn pain into purpose and heartache into hope as you...

- recognize Jesus through your scars
- remove the mask and be real
- release the power of healed wounds

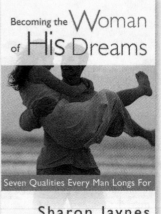

BECOMING THE WOMAN OF HIS DREAMS

Do you want to become the woman of your husband's dreams? The woman who makes him sorry to leave in the morning and eager to come home at night? If you would like a little "wow!" back in your relationship with the man you married, *Becoming the Woman of His Dreams* offers you an insightful look at the wonderful, unique, and God-ordained role only you have in your husband's life.

Includes a Bible study guide for personal or group use.

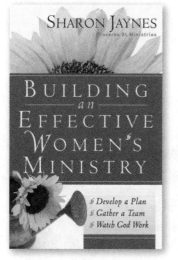

BUILDING AN EFFECTIVE WOMEN'S MINISTRY

Do you want to develop or improve a women's ministry but feel overwhelmed by the responsibility? Uncertain about where to start? Sharon Jaynes, vice president of Proverbs 31 Ministries, provides clear answers to nearly any question you can think of and presents the planning tools and confidence-builders you need to succeed. Discover how to identify your ministry's mission; develop a leadership team; avoid burnout and achieve balance; create programs that nurture, reach out, and revive; and much more!

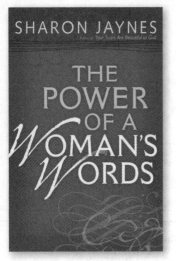

THE POWER OF A WOMAN'S WORDS

"You have incredible power in your sphere of influence with the words you speak!" Your words can...

- build courage into a husband's life
- instill confidence into a child's heart
- fire up a friend's smoldering dreams
- draw the lost to Christ

Do you want to build up, encourage, and cheer others? Or maybe you need to corral your tongue a bit more? Then this book is for you!

An easy-to-use workbook and study guide, perfect for individual or group study, is also available.

BECOMING A WOMAN WHO LISTENS TO GOD

Do you long to hear God's voice? Do you have a hard time focusing on Him because of your hectic schedule and demands on your time? Sharon understands! She offers you encouragement and practical help for hearing God's voice daily.

"I discovered that some of God's most memorable messages were delivered while men and women were right in the middle of the hustle and bustle of everyday life," Sharon shares. "He spoke to Moses while he was tending sheep, to Gideon while he was threshing wheat, to the woman at the well while she was drawing water for her housework. It is not a matter of does He speak, but will we listen."

More than a "how to" book, *Becoming a Woman Who Listens to God* is a warm, fun, tender look at recognizing the wonderful and unexpected ways God reaches out to you with His love and presence.

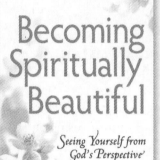

BECOMING SPIRITUALLY BEAUTIFUL

In Becoming Spiritually Beautiful, popular author Sharon Jaynes gently shares how becoming spiritually beautiful is something full of promise and possibilities. Spiritual beauty brings new beginnings, fresh faith, and the hope of a beauty unique in the universe...the beauty of a woman who

- overcomes lies about herself and sees the truth
- believes that God has a good plan for her life
- leaves the past in the past and finds peace in the present

Readers will discover that true beauty is not based on external adornments—it's really all about what goes on inside a woman. In letting God transform their hearts, minds, wills, and emotions, women will see that knowing and loving the Lord is better than anything else.